UPDATED EDITION

Guess What!

Student's Book 3A with eBook

American English

Susannah Reed with Kay Bentley
Series Editor: Lesley Koustaff

CAMBRIDGE

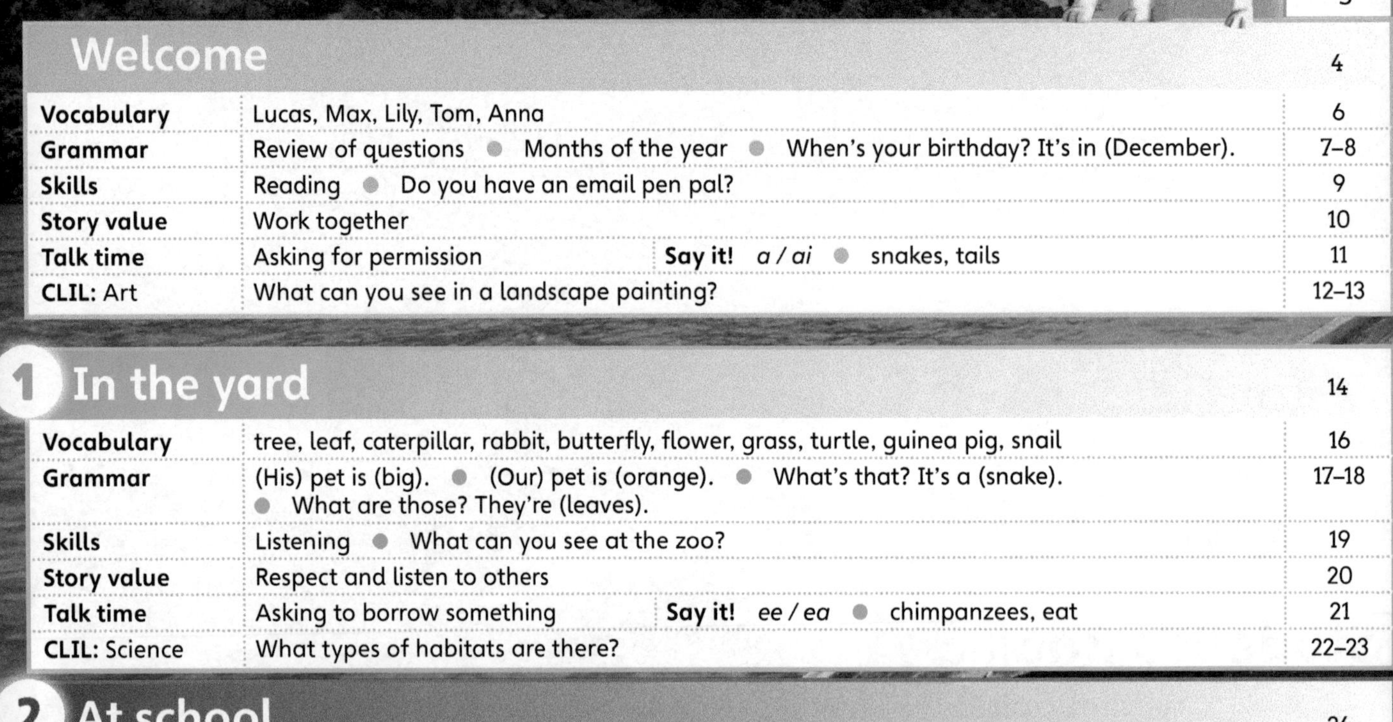

Contents

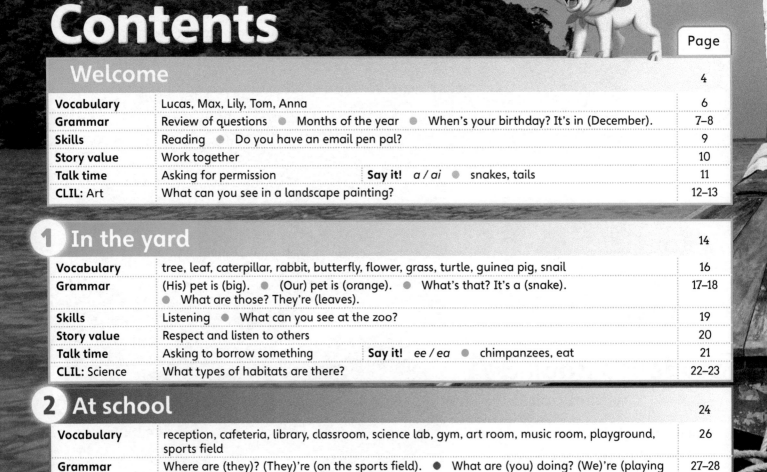

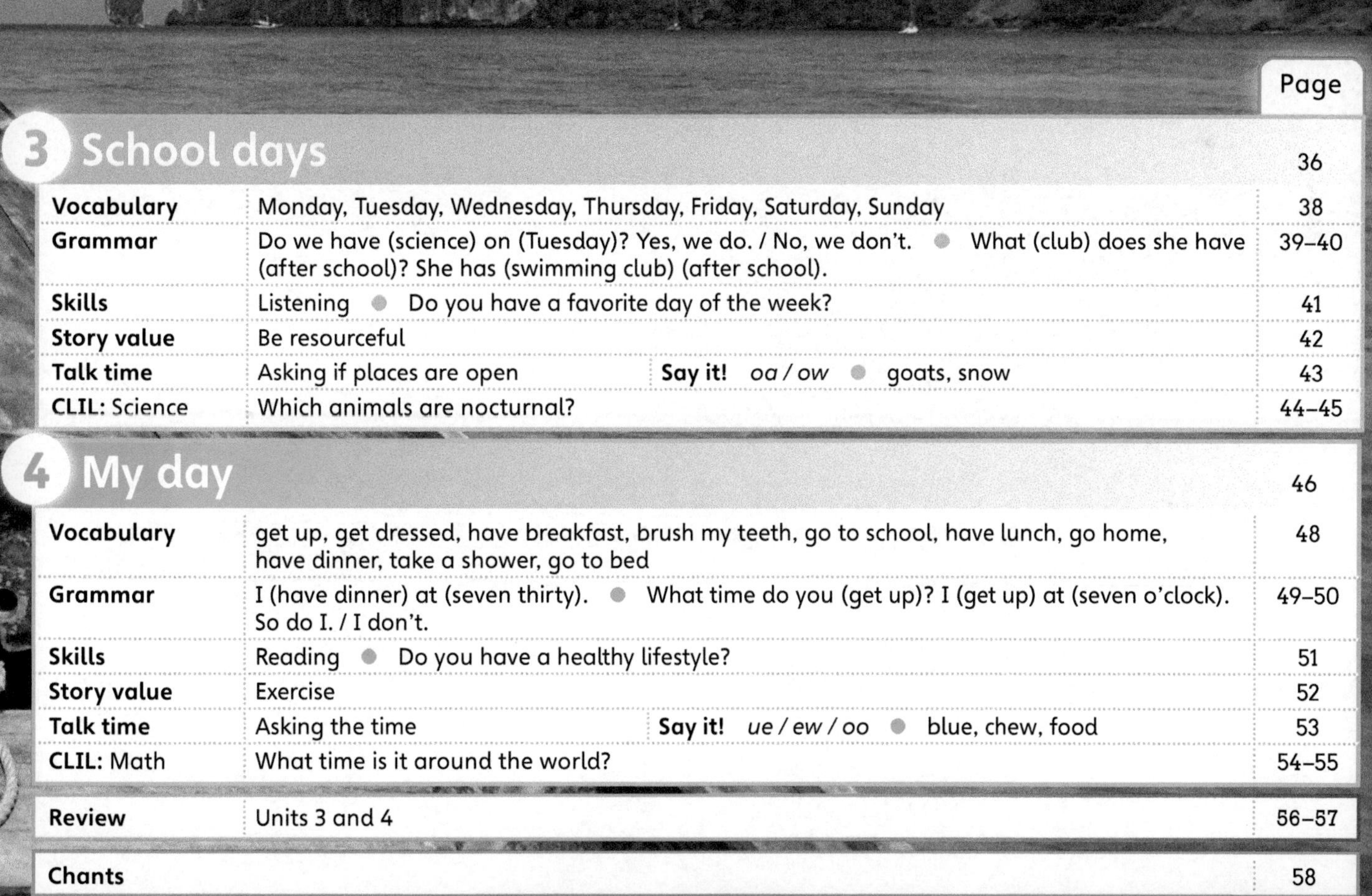

Welcome

Guess What!

1 Listen and point.

2 Listen, point, and repeat.

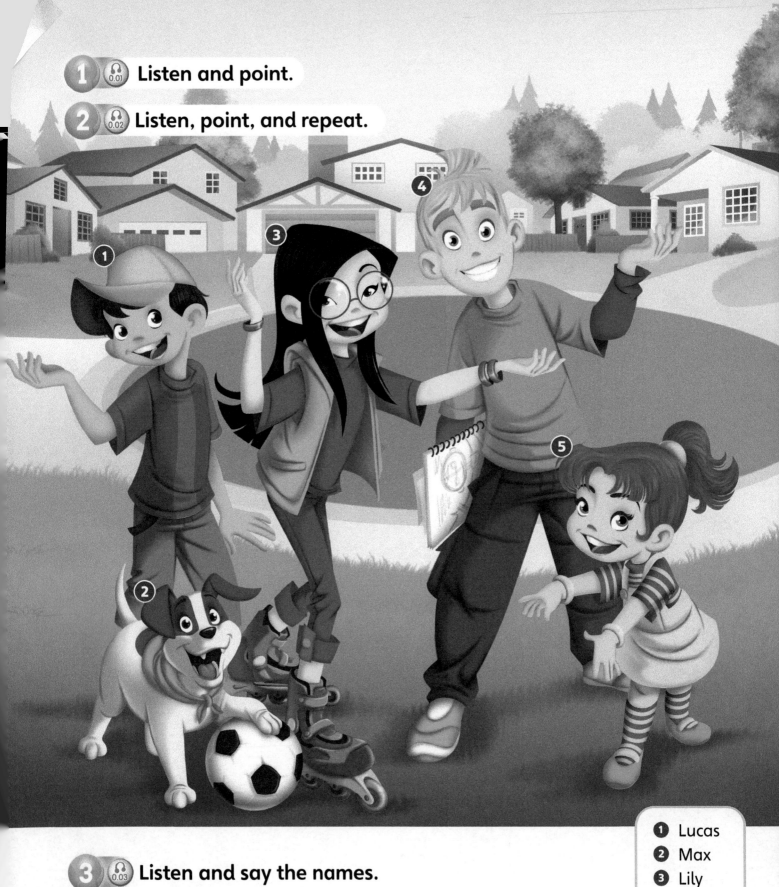

1 Lucas
2 Max
3 Lily
4 Tom
5 Anna

3 Listen and say the names.

4 Think Describe and guess who.

→ Workbook page 4

5 0.04 Sing the song.

Questions, questions,
I like asking questions.
What's your name?
How old are you?
What's your favorite color?

Questions, questions,
I like asking questions.
Do you like sports?
Do you have a pet?
Can you draw a picture of me?

Questions, questions,
I like asking questions.

6 Match the questions to the answers.

1. What's your name?
2. How old are you?
3. What's your favorite color?
4. Do you like sports?
5. Do you have a pet?
6. Can you draw a picture of me?

a Yes, I do. I have a dog.

b I'm ten years old.

c Yes, I do. My favorite sports are swimming and tennis.

d Yes, I can. I like art.

e My name's Lily.

f My favorite color is yellow.

7 About Me Ask and answer with a friend.

My favorite color is blue.

8 Listen and repeat.

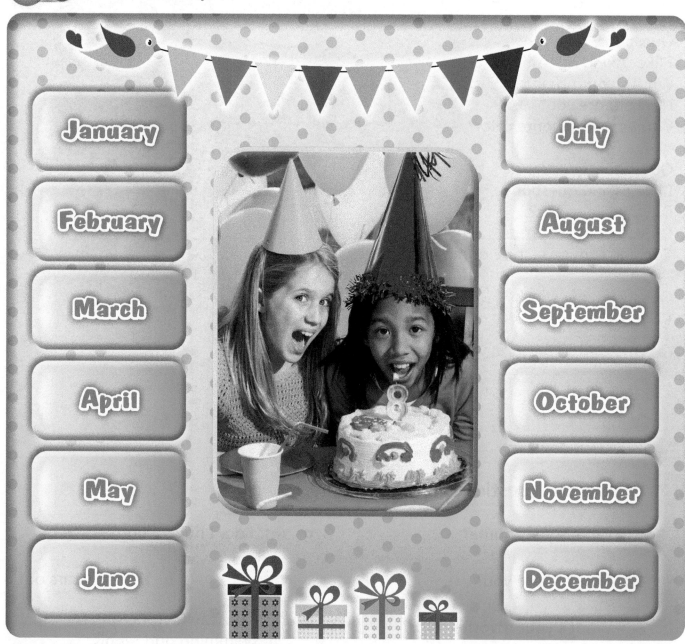

January

February

March

April

May

June

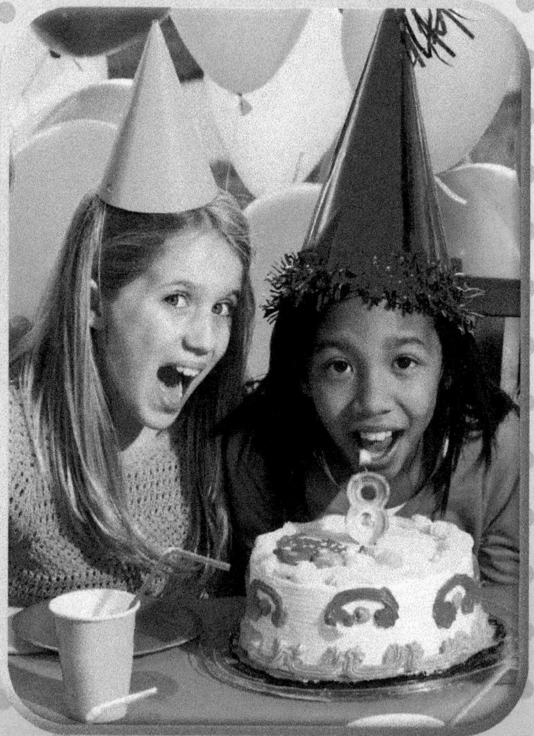

July

August

September

October

November

December

9 Listen and say the next month.

January, February, March …

April!

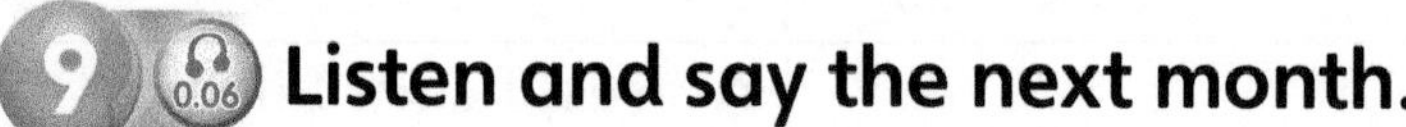

10 Ask and answer with a friend.

When's your birthday?

It's in June.

Remember!

When's your birthday?
It's in December.

11 Go to page 58. Listen and repeat the chant.

Grammar fun!

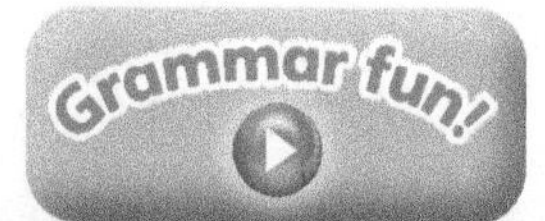

→ Workbook page 6

Skills: *Reading and speaking*

Let's start! **Do you have an email pen pal?**

12 0.08 Read and listen.

Hi. My name's Juan. I'm ten years old. My birthday is in March.

I live in a small house with my family. I have two sisters and a brother. I don't have any pets, but I like animals.

I like basketball and field hockey, but my favorite sport is baseball. I like fishing, too.

What about you?

Email me back.

Juan

13 Read again and answer the questions.

1 How old is Juan?
2 When's his birthday?
3 How many brothers does he have?
4 Does he like animals?
5 Does he like sports?

14 About Me Ask and answer with a friend.

How old are you?
Do you have any brothers or sisters?
Do you have a pet?
What's your favorite sport?

Writing

Workbook page 7: Write an email to a pen pal.

15
0.09
Story
Read and listen. Watch.
1
Happy birthday, Lily!
Thanks, Tom! Thanks everyone for your presents!
2
What's this present?
I don't know.
Open it, Lily!
3
It's a cell phone!
And look at this!
4
Treasure Hunt.
Find 7 things in 7 days.
Text 123 to join.
A surprise at the end!
5
Let's do the treasure hunt together!
Good idea.
6
Dad, can we do this treasure hunt, please?
Yes, of course! It sounds fun.
123 – there!
Value: Work together

→ Workbook page 8

  Talk Time Listen and repeat. Then act.

fly this kite | do this treasure hunt | go to the movie theater | play outside | go to the sports center

Say it!

17 Listen and repeat.

Snakes make trails with their tails.

→ Workbook page 9

What can you see in a landscape painting?

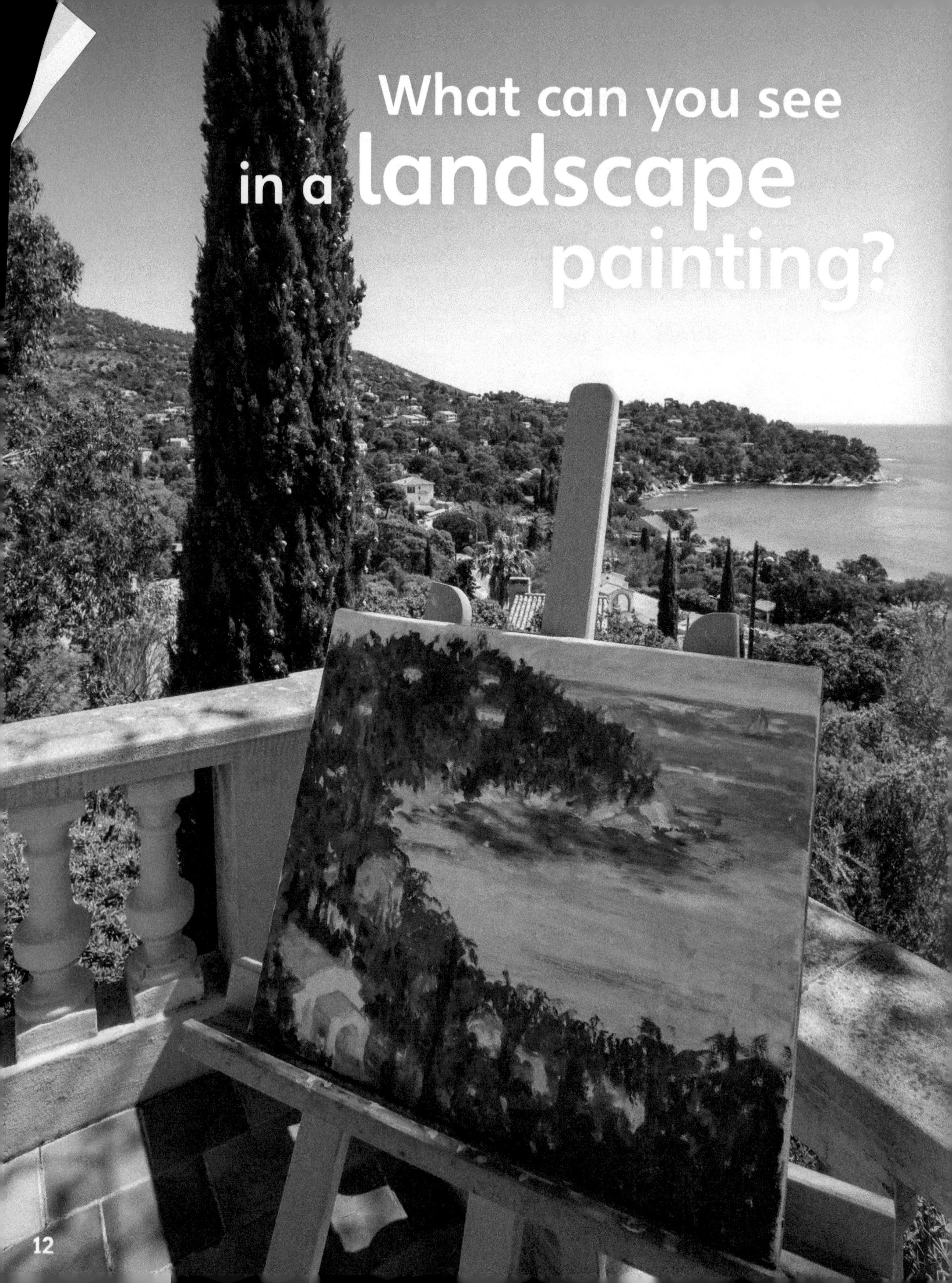

1 Listen and repeat.

river

ocean

waterfall

forest

mountain

2 Watch the video.

3 What can you see in the landscape paintings?

Guess What!

Chinese artists paint landscapes on rice paper and silk.

Let's collaborate!

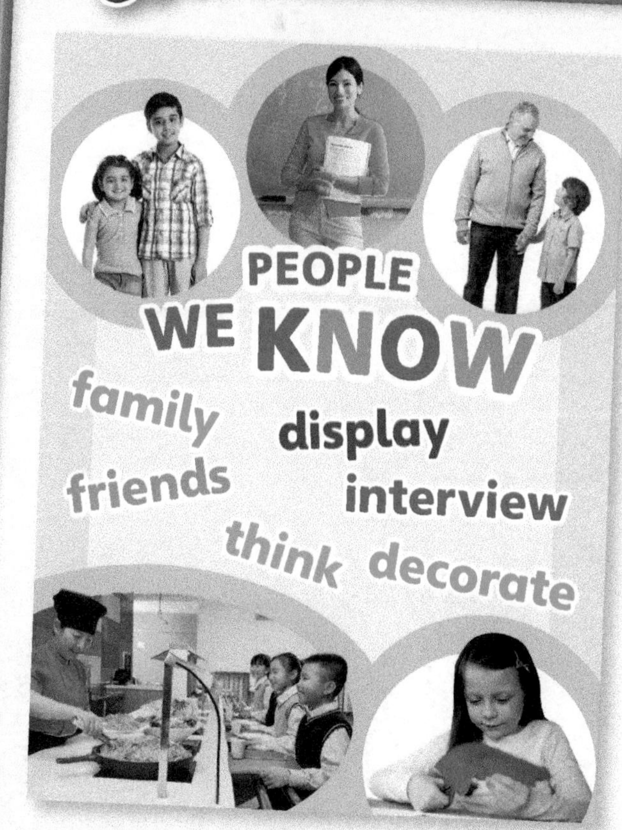

PEOPLE
WE KNOW
family
display
friends
interview
think
decorate

4 What would you like to paint in a landscape painting?

1 In the yard

Look!

Guess What!

1 Listen and point. (1.01)

2 Listen, point, and repeat. (1.02)

1. tree
2. leaf
3. caterpillar
4. rabbit
5. butterfly
6. flower
7. grass
8. turtle
9. guinea pig
10. snail

3 Listen and say the words. (1.03)

4 Think Describe and guess what.

It's a plant. It's green.

Grass!

→ Workbook page 12

5 Sing the song.

My pet is white.
Your pet is gray.
Our pets aren't big,
They're small.
Where are our pets?
Can you see our pets?

Her pet is white.
His pet is gray.
Their pets aren't big,
They're small.
Where are their pets?
Can you see their pets?

Where are our pets?
Can you see their pets?

6 Read and match. Then say the animal.

1 
My pet is big and black.

2 
Her pet is small and orange.

3 
Our pet is small and yellow.

4 
Their pet is gray and beautiful.

a 

b 

c 

d 

7 Look at the photographs. Ask and answer with a friend.

Number 3. Is their pet a bird?

Yes, it is.

Remember!
His pet is big.
Our pet is orange.

Grammar fun!

8 1.05 Listen and repeat.

9 1.06 Listen and say the numbers.

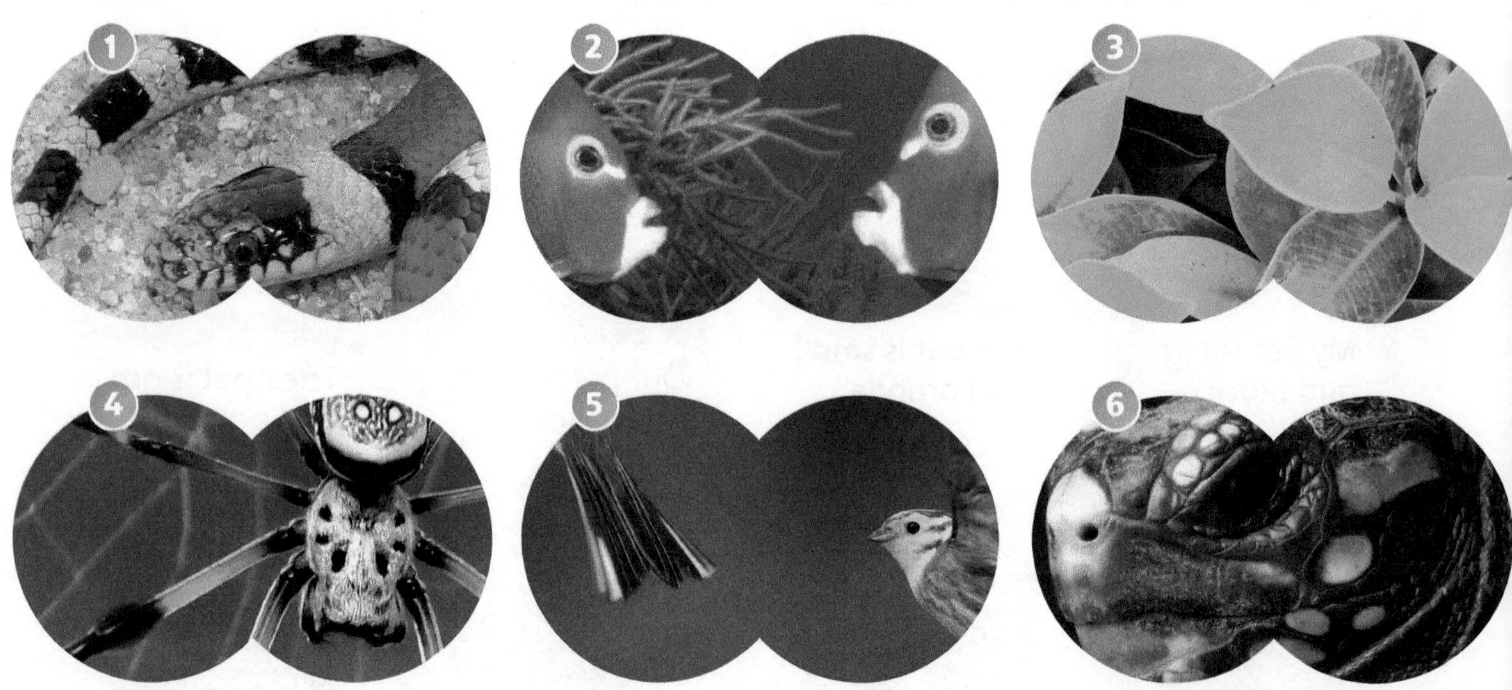

10 Look at the photographs. Ask and answer with a friend.

11 1.07 Go to page 58. Listen and repeat the chant.

Remember!

What's that?
It's a snake.
What are those?
They're leaves.

→ Workbook page 14

Skills: *Listening and speaking*

What can you see at the zoo?

12 Listen and match.

House of bugs

a

b

c

d

13 Listen again and say *true* or *false*.

1 Lucy likes snails.
2 Ryan likes ants.
3 Sara doesn't like the butterfly.
4 Jake doesn't like caterpillars.

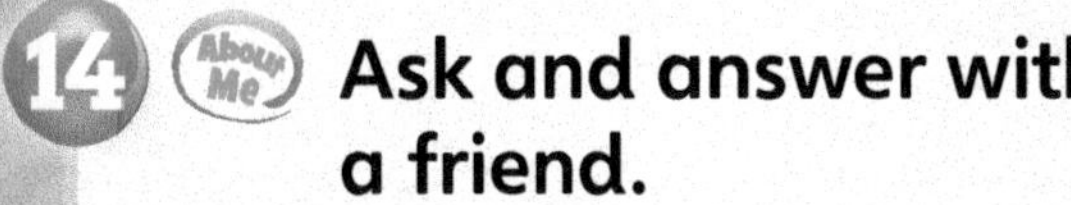

14 Ask and answer with a friend.

What is your favorite bug?
What color is it?
What bugs can you see outside?

Writing

Workbook page 15: Write about your favorite bug.

15 1.10 Story Read and listen. Watch.

1
What's that?
Max loves soccer.
It's a message!

2
Find a toy tiger.

3
A toy tiger? Where?
Can I help?
Not now, Anna.

6
Wait! Is this your tiger, Anna?
Yes, it is.
Can we borrow it, please?

7
Yes, you can! Here you are.
Thank you, Anna.
Sorry, Anna. Thank you.

 Value: Respect and listen to others

→ Workbook page 16

16 Listen and repeat. Then act.

computer game toy car eraser camera book

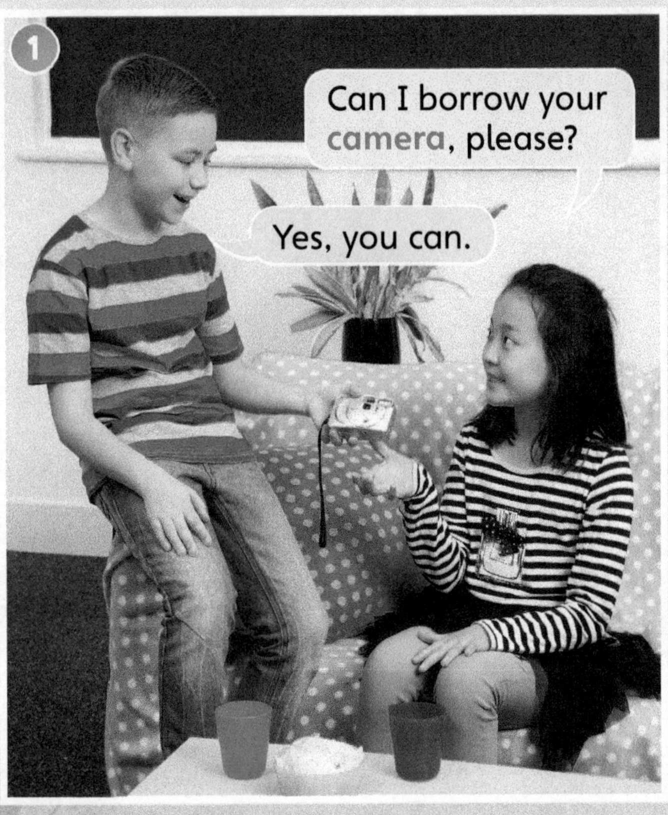

1
Can I borrow your camera, please?
Yes, you can.

2
Can I borrow your book, please?
No, I'm sorry, you can't.

Say it!

17 Listen and repeat.

Chimpanzees eat and sleep in trees.

What types of habitats are there?

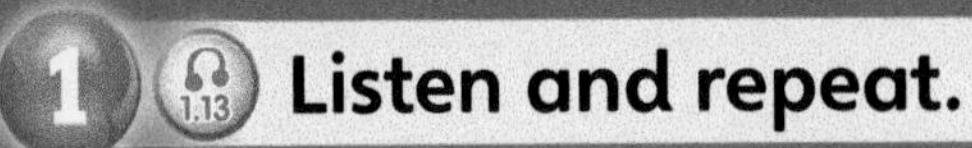

desert

rain forest

grassland

tundra

2 CLIL Watch the video.

3 Match the habitats with the groups of animals.

1
monkey
crocodile
snake

2
lion
giraffe
snake

desert
grassland
rainforest
tundra

3
spider
snake
camel

4
goat
sheep
bear

4 What type of habitat would you like to visit?

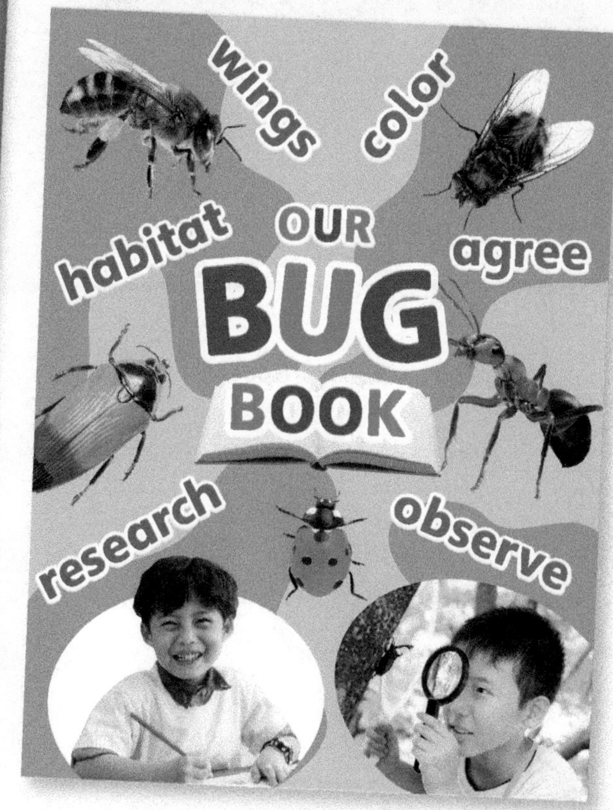

Let's collaborate!
wings
color
habitat
OUR BUG BOOK
agree
research
observe

→ Workbook page 18

2 At school

Look!

SCHOOL BUS
117
Guess What!

1 Listen and point.

2 Listen, point, and repeat.

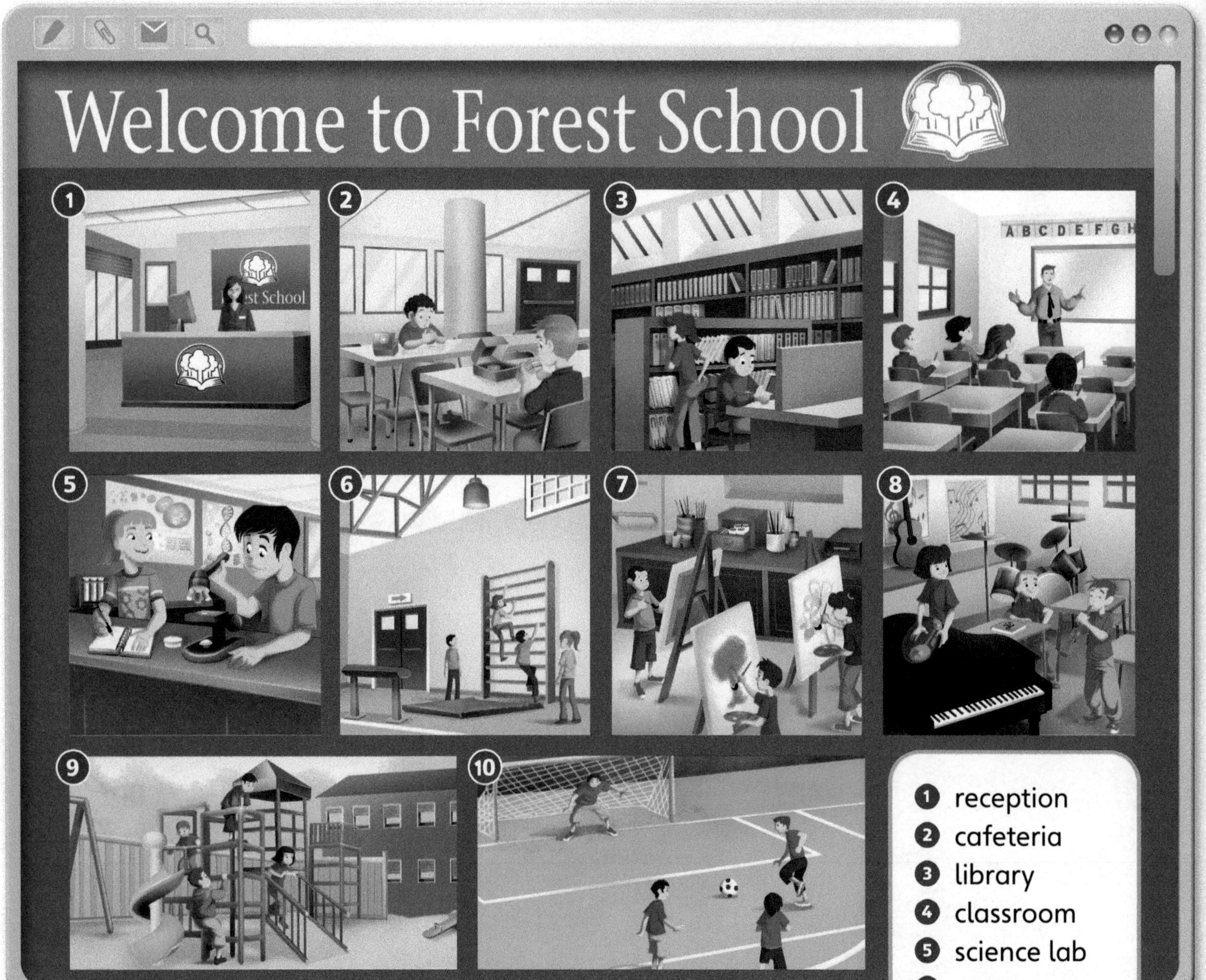

Welcome to Forest School

1 reception
2 cafeteria
3 library
4 classroom
5 science lab
6 gym
7 art room
8 music room
9 playground
10 sports field

3 Listen and say the places.

4 Describe and guess where.

This is Lily's favorite room.

Music room!

→ Workbook page 20

5 2.04 Sing the song.

Dave and Daisy, where are you?
We're in the cafeteria.
Where are Dave and Daisy?
They're in the cafeteria.

Max and Mary, where are you?
We're in the music room.
Where are Max and Mary?
They're in the music room.

Sam and Susie, where are you?
We're on the sports field.
Where are Sam and Susie?
They're on the sports field.

6 Read and match.

a We're in the art room.

b We're on the playground.

c We're in the library.

7 Look at the pictures in activities 5 and 6. Ask and answer with a friend.

Where are they?

They're on the playground.

Remember!

Where are they?
They're on the sports field.

→ Workbook page 21

8 Listen and repeat.

9 Look and find. Then listen and say the numbers.

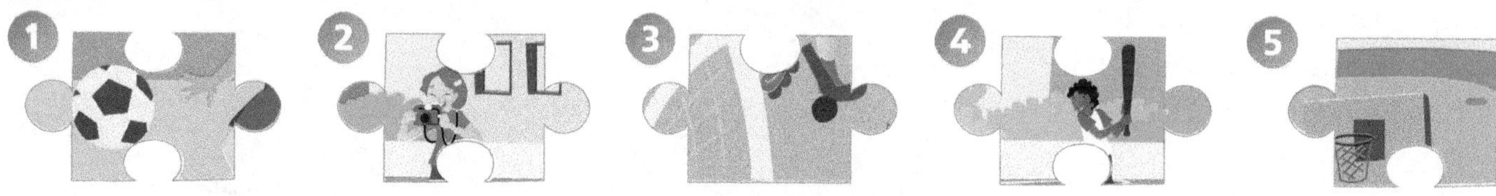

10 Look at the picture. Ask and answer with a friend.

What are they doing?

They're playing baseball.

Remember!

What are you doing?
We're playing baseball.

11 Go to page 58. Listen and repeat the chant.

Skills: *Reading and speaking*

What places can you find in your school?

12 Read and listen. Then match.

1 My name's Lisa. Can you find a photograph of me? I'm standing outside my school. My school is big.

2 This is the playground. It's a big playground. Some children are playing a game of basketball. I like basketball, but my favorite sport is tennis.

3 This is a classroom. There's a board and some desks and chairs. These children are doing math. I like math, but my favorite class is art. I like drawing and painting.

4 This is my favorite room. It's our school library. There are lots of books, and I like reading. There are a lot of children in the library today.

a

b

c

d

13 Read again and answer the questions.

1 Is Lisa's school big or small?
2 What is Lisa's favorite sport?
3 What are the children in the classroom doing?
4 Does Lisa like reading?

14 Make sentences about your school. Say *true* or *false*.

Our school is small.

False. It's big.

Writing

Workbook page 23: Write a description of your school.

15 2.09 Story Read and listen. Watch.

Value: Keep your environment clean

→ Workbook page 24

 **Listen and repeat. Then act.**

pick up this litter   clean the living room   play nicely
put those toys in your room

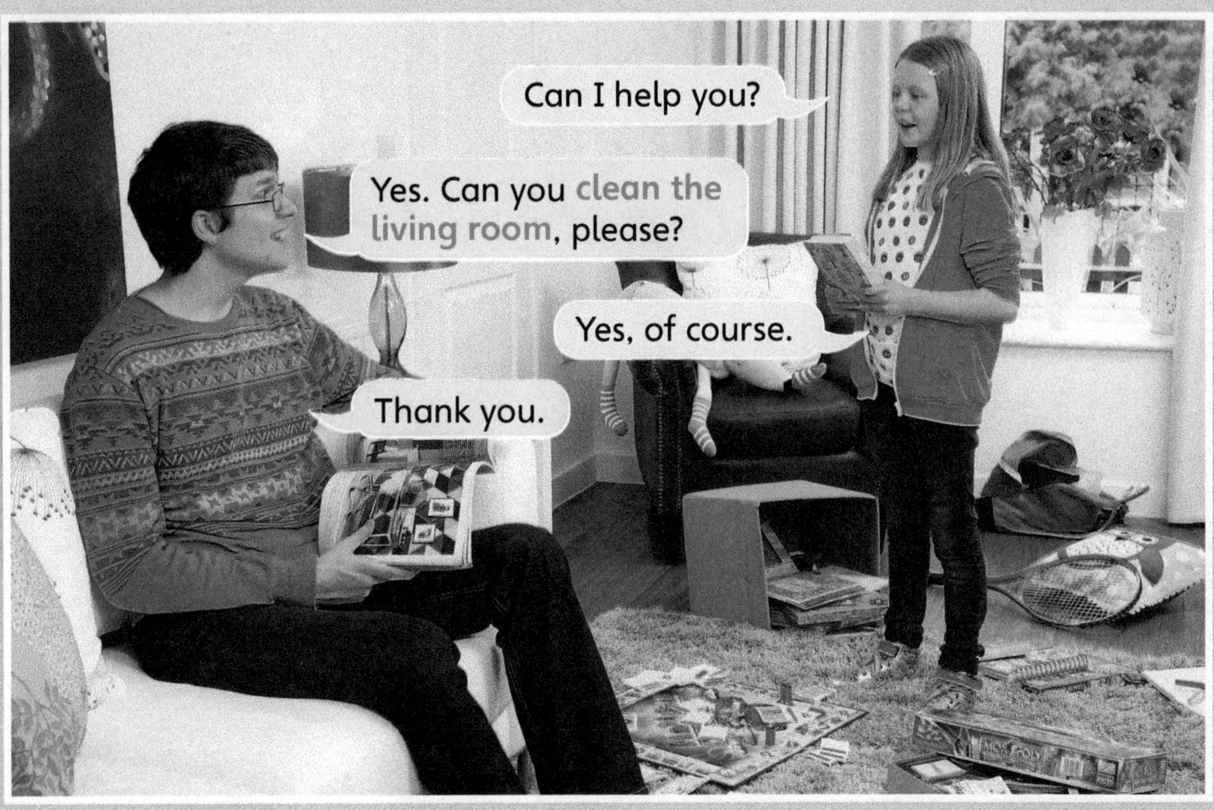

Can I help you?
Yes. Can you clean the living room, please?
Yes, of course.
Thank you.

Say it!

17 2.11 **Listen and repeat.**

Tigers sometimes fight at night.

→ Workbook page 25

What materials can we recycle?

1 Listen and repeat. 2.12

1 recycling bin

2 paper

3 can

4 bottle

5 cardboard

2 CLIL Watch the video.

Guess What!
We can make recycled paper into paint.

3 What can you recycle?

Let's collaborate!

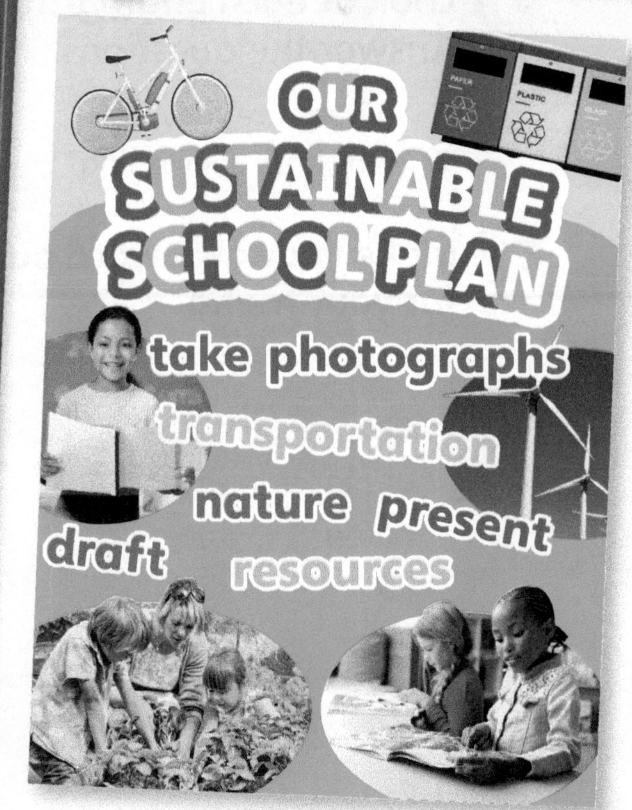

4 What materials does your school recycle?

→ Workbook page 26

Review

Units 1 and 2

1 **Find the months in the word puzzles.**

2 2.13 **Listen and match the months to the photographs.**

3 **Look at each photograph. Answer the questions.**

1 Where are they?
2 What are they doing?

4 **Make your own word puzzles for your friend.**

Choose months, nature, or places in school:

butter rary
lib fly

Carnival Day

Sports Day

Children's Day

Teacher's Day

→ Workbook pages 28–29

5 Play the game.

What's that?

It's a rabbit. Good. I have a rabbit.

What are those?

They're spiders. I don't have spiders.

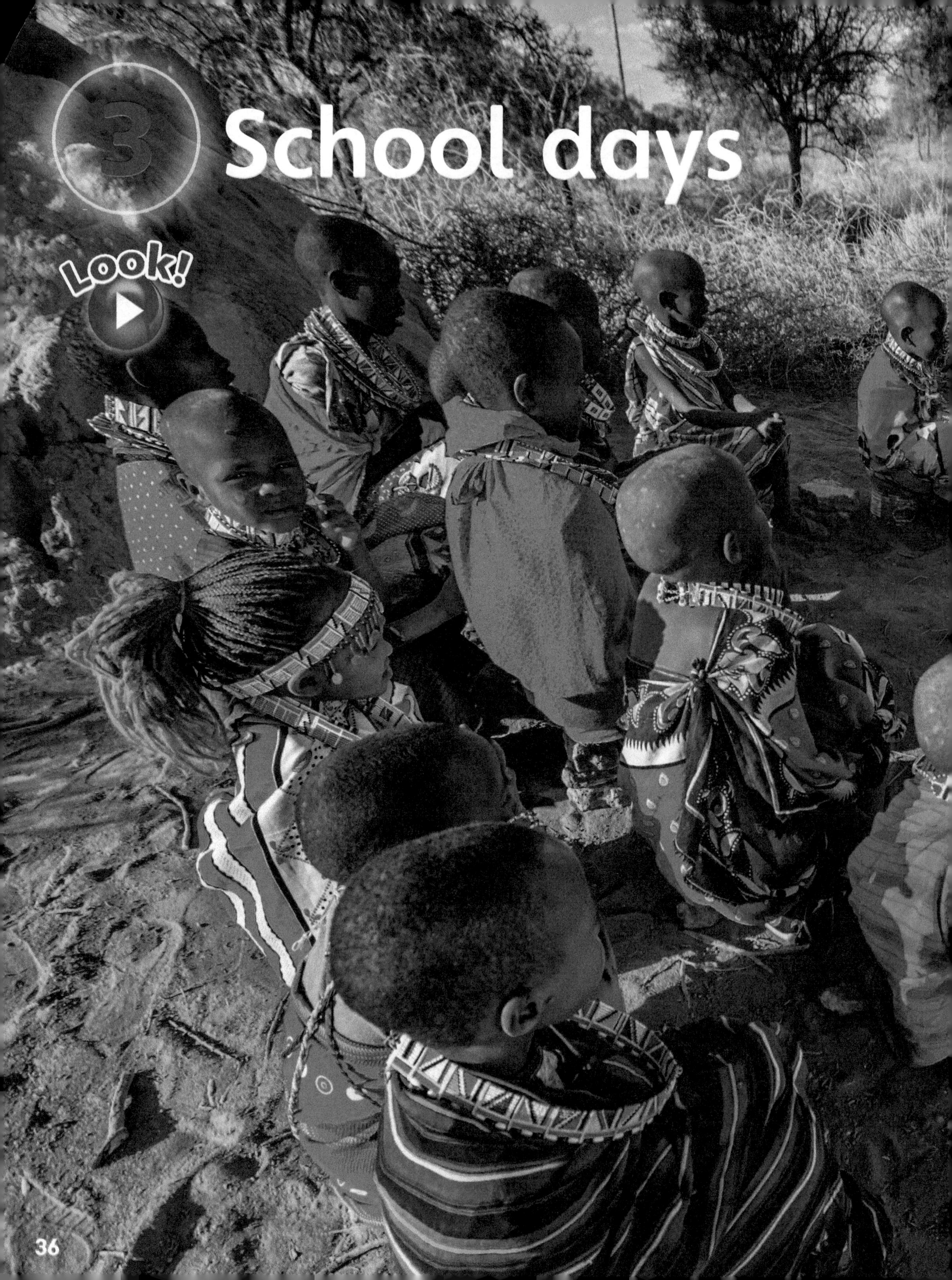
3
School days
Look!

Guess What!

1 Listen and point.

2 Listen, point, and repeat.

3 Listen and say the days.

4 Think Make sentences and guess the days.

He has math, and she has science.

Monday!

1. Monday
2. Tuesday
3. Wednesday
4. Thursday
5. Friday
6. Saturday
7. Sunday

→ Workbook page 30

5 Sing the song.

We have math on Monday.
We don't have math on Tuesday.
Do we have math on Wednesday?
Yes, we do – on Wednesday, too.
We have math on Monday and Wednesday.

We have English on Thursday.
We don't have English on Friday.
Do we have English on Monday?
Yes, we do – on Monday, too.
We have English on Monday and Thursday.

6 Make a schedule with a friend. Ask and answer.

7 Make sentences about your schedule. Say *true* or *false*.

We have music on Monday and Friday.

False!

We don't have music on Wednesday.

True!

Remember!

Do we have science on Tuesday?
Yes, we do. No, we don't.

→ Workbook page 31

8 Listen and look. Then listen and repeat.

in the morning

lunchtime

in the afternoon

dinnertime

after school

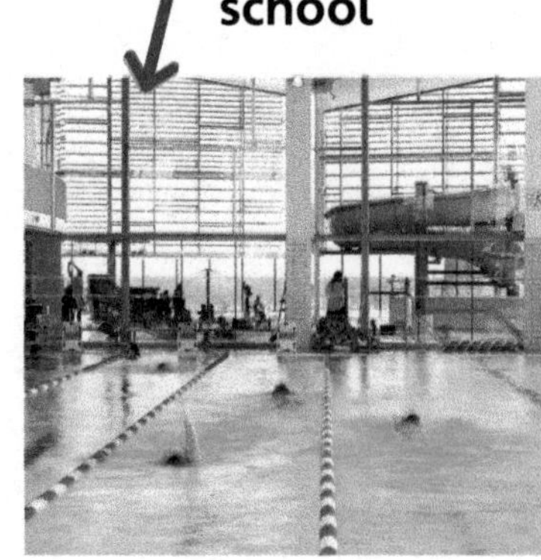

9 Now read and answer the questions.

1 What classes does Amy have in the morning?
2 What classes does Amy have in the afternoon?
3 What club does Amy have after school?
4 What class does Amy have before lunch?
5 What class does Amy have after lunch?

Amy has math and English in the morning.

  Choose a day from your schedule. Play a guessing game.

What do you have in the morning?

I have math and science.

Is it Wednesday?

Yes, it is.

 Go to page 58. Listen and repeat the chant.

Remember!

What club **does she have** after school?
She has swimming club after school.

→ Workbook page 32

Skills: *Reading and speaking*

Do you have a favorite day of the week?

12 Listen and choose.

Favorite day
Sunday

Morning
Swimming competition

Afternoon
Art club

Evening
Movie theater trip

Favorite day
Friday

Morning
Math test

Afternoon
Field trip to a farm

Evening
Field hockey club

Favorite day
Saturday

Morning
Art competition

Afternoon
Movie theater trip

Evening
Dance club

13 Listen again and say *true* or *false*.

1. Caleb's favorite class is math.
2. Salima's favorite class is music.
3. Maddie likes playing field hockey.
4. Salima likes dancing.

14 Ask and answer with a friend.

What's your favorite class?
What clubs do you have after school?
Do you like competitions?
Do you like school tests?

Writing

Workbook page 33: Write about your favorite day.

15 3.09 Story

Read and listen. Watch.

1 Find this painting.

2
What day is today?
It's Saturday.
Great! I like art. Let's go to the art gallery.

3
Is the art gallery open on Saturdays?
Yes, it is.
Come on. Let's go!

4
OK. Here we are.
Now where's the painting?
Over there!

5
What can we do now?
We can't take a photograph of the painting.
I have an idea!

6
Be careful!
Are you OK, Tom?
Yes, I'm fine. Don't worry.

7
It's very good, Tom.
What do you think, Max?

Value: Be resourceful

→ Workbook page 34

16 Listen and repeat. Then act.

art gallery | hospital | sports center | movie theater | library

1
Is the movie theater open on Sundays?
Yes, it is.
EVENT MOVIES

2
Is the library open on Mondays in the afternoon?
No, it isn't. It's closed.
connect
Love your Library
Open your world

Say it!

17 Listen and repeat.

Goats need warm coats in the snow.

goat

→ Workbook page 35

Which animals are nocturnal?

1 Listen and repeat. 3.12

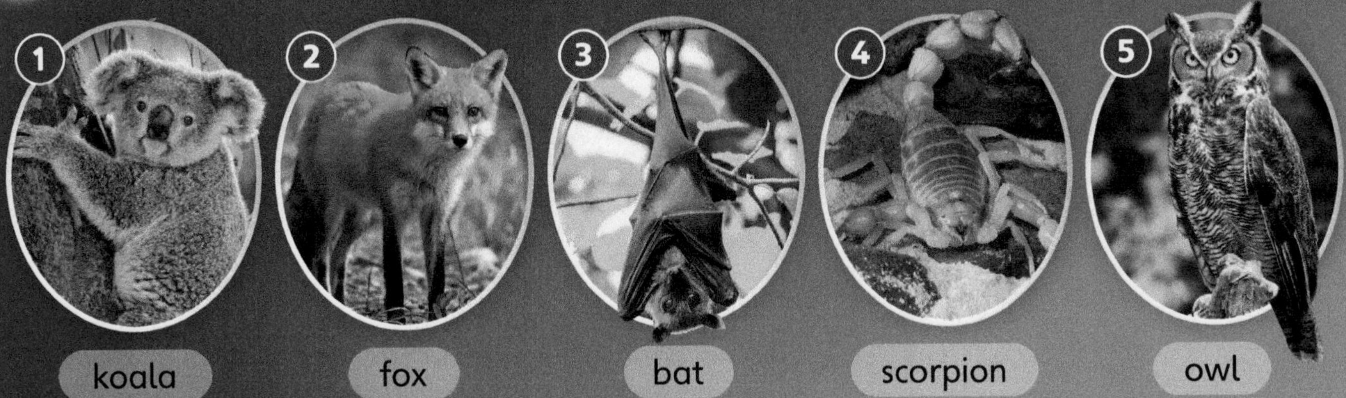

koala fox bat scorpion owl

2 CLIL Watch the video.

Guess What!
At night, owls can see mice 18 m in front of them.

3 Which animals are nocturnal?

4 Which animals in your country are nocturnal?

Let's collaborate!

OUR
FAVORITE
SCHOOL DAYS BLOG
make notes
design
plan
school
activities
home

→ Workbook page 36

4 My day

Guess What!

1 Listen and point.

2 Listen, point, and repeat.

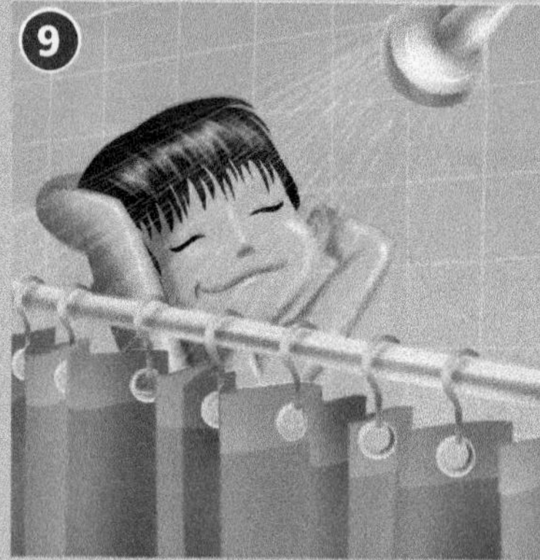

1. get up
2. get dressed
3. have breakfast
4. brush my teeth
5. go to school
6. have lunch
7. go home
8. have dinner
9. take a shower
10. go to bed

3 Listen and say the numbers.

4 Say the actions and guess the numbers.

Go home.

Number 7!

→ Workbook page 38

5 4.04 Sing the song.

I get up at eight o'clock.
I have breakfast at eight thirty.
I go to school at nine o'clock,
And I have lunch at twelve thirty.
Hey, hey, every day.

I go home at three thirty,
And I play with my friends.
I have dinner at seven thirty.
I go to bed at nine o'clock at night.
Hey, hey, every day.

6 4.05 Listen and say the names.

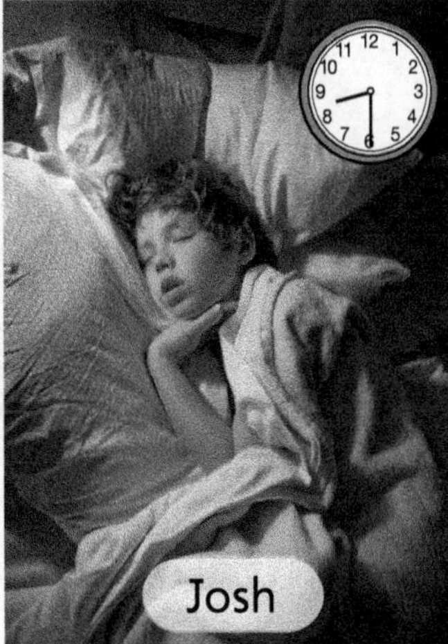

7 About Me Make sentences about your day. Say *true* or *false*.

I have breakfast at twelve thirty.

False!

Remember!

I have dinner at seven thirty.
I go to bed at nine o'clock.

8 Listen and repeat.

What time do you have breakfast?
I have breakfast at eight o'clock.
So do I.
I don't. I have breakfast at seven thirty.

9 Listen and answer.

1
2
3
4

10 Ask and answer with two friends.

What time do you go to school?

I go to school at nine o'clock.

So do I.

I don't. I go to school at eight thirty.

11 Go to page 58. Listen and repeat the chant.

Remember!

What time do you get up?
I get up at seven o'clock.
So do I. I don't.

Grammar fun!

Skills: *Reading and speaking*

Let's start! Do you have a healthy lifestyle?

12 4.09 Read and listen. Then answer the questionnaire.

		A	B
1	Do you get up early?	Yes, I do.	No, I don't.
2	Do you have breakfast every day?	Yes, I do.	No, I don't.
3	Do you brush your teeth in the morning and in the evening?	Yes, I do.	No, I don't.
4	Do you walk or ride your bike to school?	Yes, I do.	No, I don't.
5	Do you play outside with your friends?	Yes, I do.	No, I don't.
6	Do you like eating fruits and vegetables?	Yes, I do.	No, I don't.
7	Do you like drinking water or milk?	Yes, I do.	No, I don't.
8	Do you go to bed early?	Yes, I do.	No, I don't.

Mostly As – Good job! You have a healthy lifestyle.
Mostly Bs – Hmm! What can you do to be more healthy?

13  Now ask and answer with a friend.

Do you get up early?

Yes, I do. I get up at seven thirty.

Writing

 Workbook page 41: Write your own questionnaire.

14 4.10 Story Read and listen. Watch.

→ Workbook page 42

15 Listen and repeat. Then act.

five o'clock | four thirty | nine thirty | eight o'clock

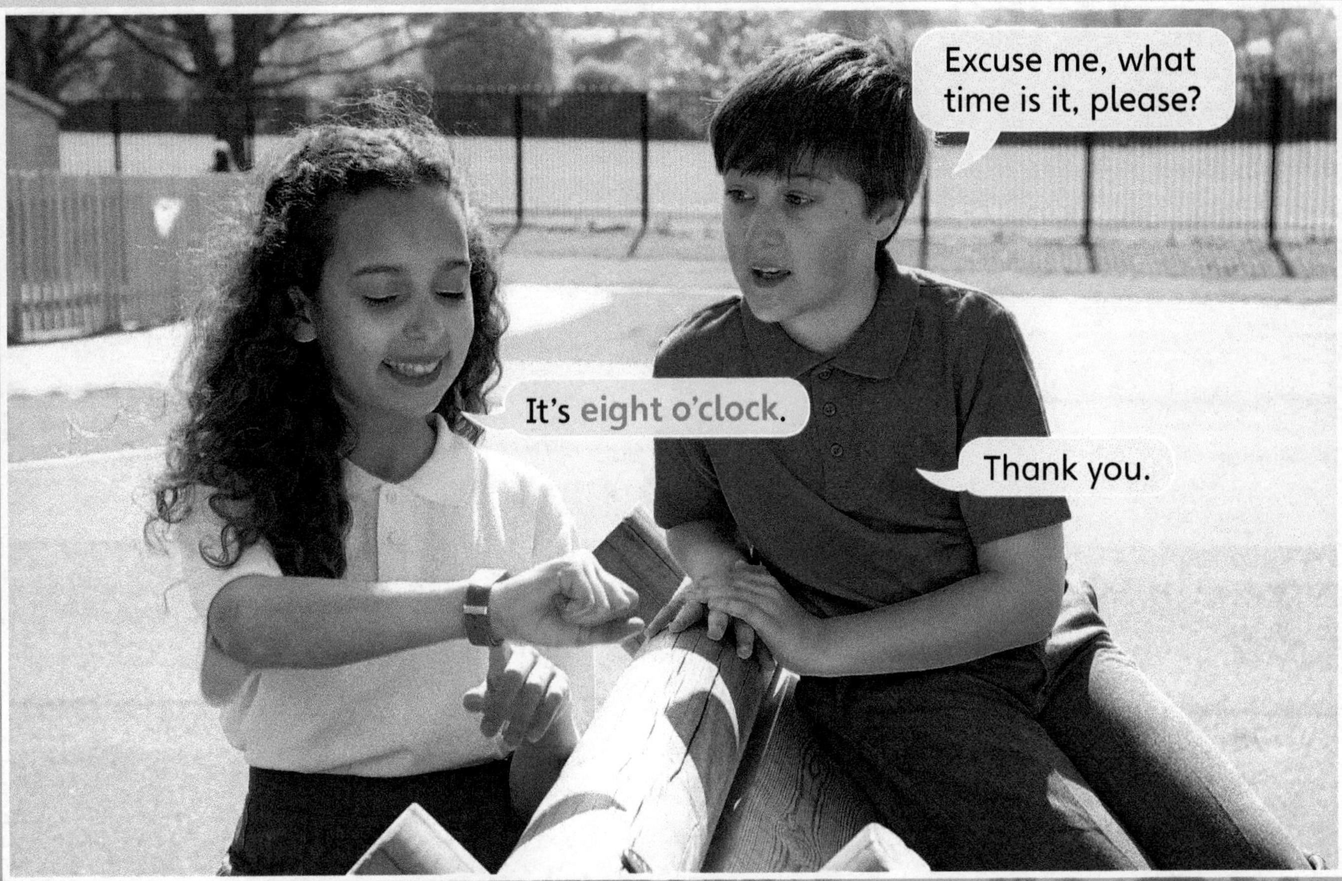

Excuse me, what time is it, please?

It's eight o'clock.

Thank you.

Say it!

16 Listen and repeat.

Blue whales don't chew their food.

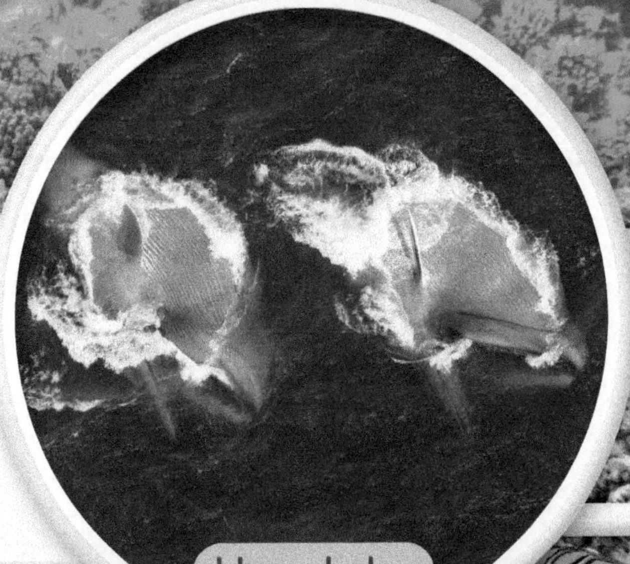

→ Workbook page 43

What time is it around the world?

1 Listen and repeat. 4.13

twelve o'clock

sixteen fifteen

ten thirty

twenty-three forty-five

2 CLIL Watch the video.

Guess What! *Brazil has three different time zones.*

3 Match the pictures with the cities on page 54. What time is it?

1 

2 

3 

4 

4 What time is it in your country?

Let's collaborate!

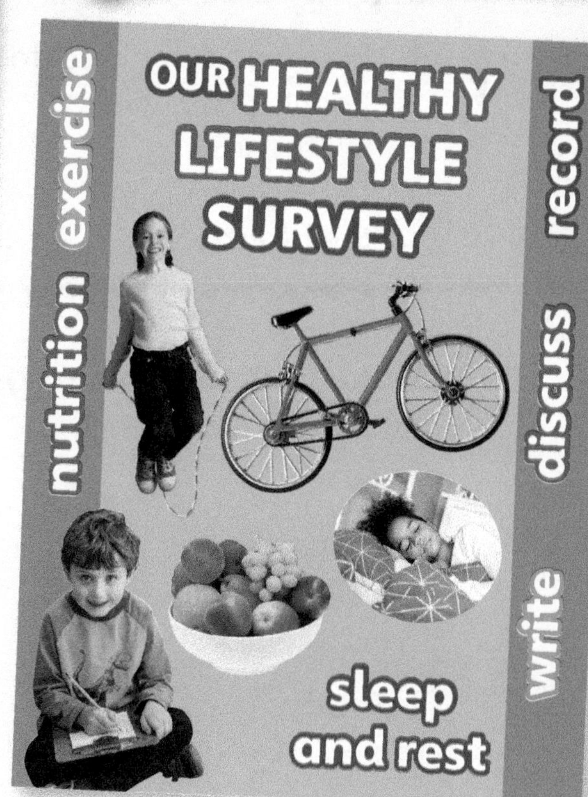

OUR HEALTHY LIFESTYLE SURVEY
nutrition
exercise
record
discuss
write
sleep and rest

Review
Units 3 and 4

1 Find the words in the puzzles and match to the photographs.

g* t* b*d

h*v* br**kf*st

pl*y t*nn*s

g* t* *rt cl*b

2 4.14 Listen and say the numbers.

3 Read Clara's sentences and say *true* or *false*.

1 I have eggs for breakfast.
2 I play soccer with my friends.
3 I have art club in the afternoon.
4 I go to bed at home.

4 Make your own word puzzles for your friend.

Choose days of the week or daily activities:
S*nd*y
T**sd*y

→ Workbook pages 46–47

5 Play the game.

Yellow

What time do you (get up)?
I (get up) at (seven thirty).

Green

What do you have on (Monday) in the (morning)?
I have (English) at (nine o'clock).

Chants

Welcome (page 8)

Listen and repeat the chant.

When's your birthday?
It's in June.
January, February, and March,
April, May, and June.

When's your birthday?
It's in December.
July, August, and September,
October, November, and December.

Unit 1 (page 18)

Listen and repeat the chant.

What's that?
It's a snail.
What are those?
They're butterflies.

What's that?
It's a snake.
What are those?
They're leaves.

Unit 2 (page 28)

Listen and repeat the chant.

What are you doing?
We're playing tennis.
What are they doing?
They're playing tennis.

What are you doing?
We're playing baseball.
What are they doing?
They're playing baseball.

Unit 3 (page 40)

Listen and repeat the chant.

What class does she have after lunch?
She has art after lunch.
What class does she have after lunch?
She has art.

What club does she have after school?
She has swimming club after school.
What club does she have after school?
She has swimming club.

Unit 4 (page 50)

Listen and repeat the chant.

What time do you have breakfast?
I have breakfast at eight o'clock.
So do I.
I don't.
I have breakfast at seven thirty.

What time do you go to school?
I go to school at nine o'clock.
So do I.
I don't.
I go to school at eight thirty.

UPDATED EDITION

Guess What!

Workbook 3 A
with Digital Pack

Contents

Lynne Marie Robertson
Series Editor: Lesley Koustaff

Welcome

1 Look and write the names.

Anna Lily ~~Lucas~~ Max Tom

1 Lucas
2 ______
3 ______
4 ______
5 ______

2 Look at activity 1. Read and write *true* or *false*.

1 Tom likes art. true
2 Anna is ten. ______
3 Max is Lucas's dog. ______
4 Lily's favorite sport is soccer. ______
5 Lucas's favorite color is red. ______

My picture dictionary  Go to page 48: Find and write the new words.

3 Read and match.

1 What's your name?
2 How old are you?
3 What's your favorite color?
4 Do you like dogs?
5 Do you have a bike?
6 Can you ride a horse?

a I'm nine years old.
b My favorite color is green.
c My name's Bill.
d Yes, I can.
e Yes, I do.
f No, I don't.

4 About Me Answer the questions. Then draw your picture.

1 What's your name?

My name is ____________________

2 How old are you?

____

3 Do you have a bike?

____

4 What's your favorite color?

____

____

5 Do you like dogs?

____

6 Can you play tennis?

____

5 Write the months in order. Then answer the question. Use the letters in the boxes to complete the answer.

1 J a n u a r y

2 F [_] _ _ _ _ _ _

3 M _ _ _ _

4 A _ _ _ _

5 M _ _

6 J _ _ [_]

7 J _ [_] _

8 A _ _ _ _ _

9 S _ _ _ _ _ _ _ _

10 O _ [_] _ _ _ _

11 N _ [_] _ _ _ _ _

12 D _ _ _ _ _ _ _

How many months are there?

_ w _ _ _ _

6 About Me Answer the questions.

1 What month is it?

It is ______________________

2 What's your favorite month?

____

My picture dictionary → Go to page 48: Find and write the new words.

Skills: *Writing*

7 Read the email. Circle the answers to the questions.

Hello!
My name's Jill. I'm eleven years old. My birthday is in April.
I have one brother and one sister. I have a pet rabbit.
My favorite sport is basketball. What about you?
Jill ☺

1 How old are you?
2 When is your birthday?
3 Do you have any brothers or sisters?
4 Do you have a pet?
5 What's your favorite sport?

8 About Me Look at activity 7. Answer the questions for you.

1 *I'm* ______________________
2 ______________________
3 ______________________
4 ______________________
5 ______________________

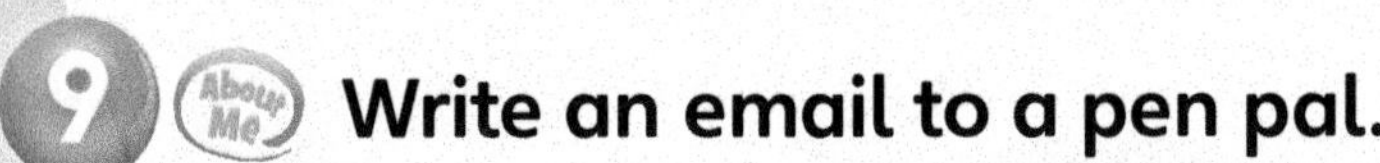

9 About Me Write an email to a pen pal.

Hello! ______________________
My name's ______________________
____
____
____
____

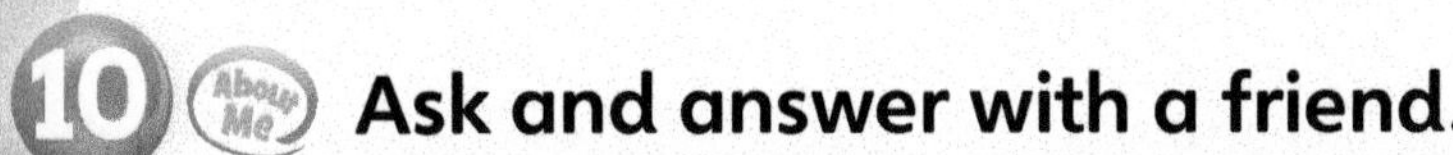

10 About Me Ask and answer with a friend.

How old are you?

I'm eleven years old.

11 Read and number in order.

a
Let's do the treasure hunt together!
Good idea.

b
Treasure Hunt.
Find 7 things in 7 days.
Text 123 to join.
A surprise at the end!

c
It's a cell phone!
And look at this!

d
Happy birthday, Lily!
Thanks, Tom. Thanks everyone for your presents!
1

e
What's this present?
I don't know.
Open it, Lily!

f
Dad, can we do this treasure hunt, please?
Yes, of course! It sounds fun.
123 – there!

12 Look at activity 11. Write *yes* or *no*.

1 It's Tom's birthday. ___no___
2 The present is a cell phone. ______
3 The treasure hunt is to find 7 things in 5 days. ______
4 Lily's friends don't want to do the treasure hunt. ______
5 The treasure hunt sounds fun. ______

13 Read and check the sentences that show the value: work together.

1 Let's do the treasure hunt together. ✓

2 Let's find my dog. ☐

3 I like card games. ☐

4 Good idea. ☐

5 Let's clean up. ☐

6 I'm playing basketball. ☐

14 Circle the words that sound like *snake*.

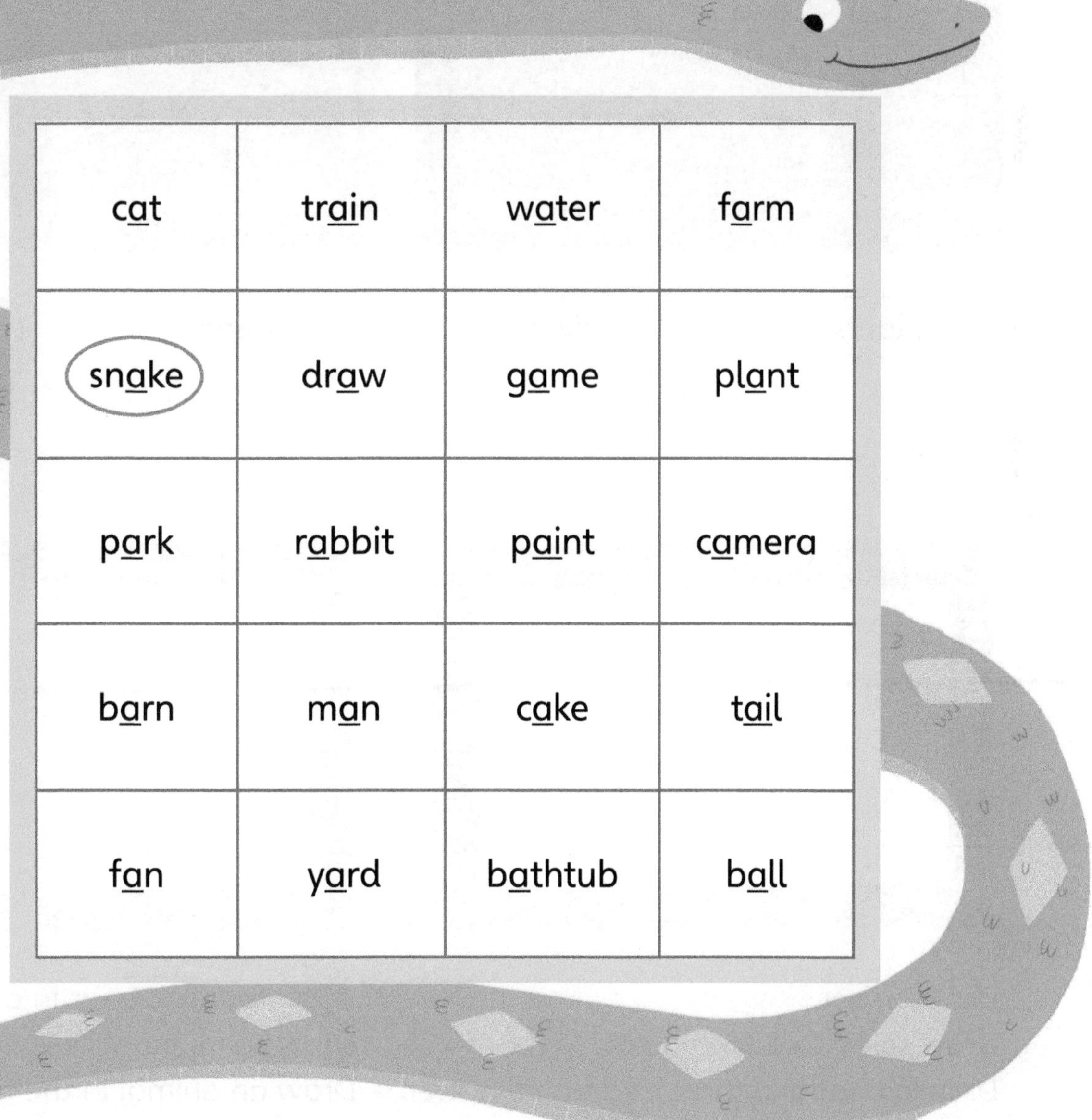

cat	train	water	farm
snake	draw	game	plant
park	rabbit	paint	camera
barn	man	cake	tail
fan	yard	bathtub	ball

What can you see in a landscape painting?

1 **Look and match.**

birds boat forest mountain

plants river ocean waterfall

1

2

Draw a river.
Draw some trees behind it.
Draw a boat and three ducks on the river.

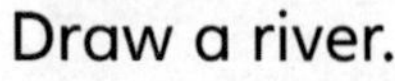

Draw four tall trees in a forest.
Draw some plants between the trees.
Draw an animal in the forest.

Evaluation

1 Do the word puzzle.

Down ↓

1 

2 

4

Across →

3 

5

2 About Me Find and write the questions. Then answer.

1 are / old / you? / How

How old are you?

I'm

2 your / When's / birthday?

3 swim? / you / Can

4 color? / your / What's / favorite

5 you / Do / a / have / brother?

3 About Me Complete the sentences about this unit.

1 I can talk about ________ .

2 I can write about ________ .

3 My favorite part is ________ .

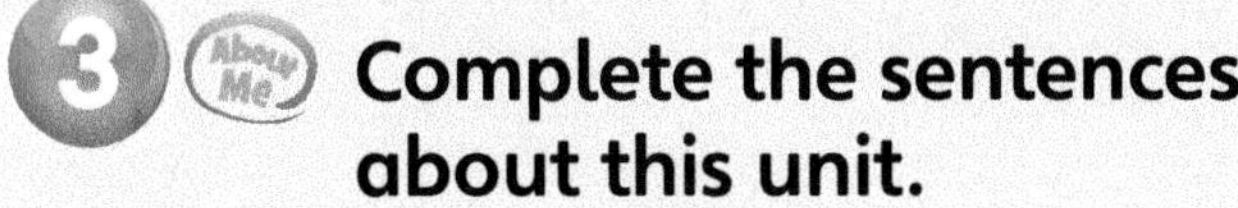

4 Puzzle Guess what it is.

Go to page 53 and circle the answer.

1 In the yard

1 Look and guess. Then find and write the words.

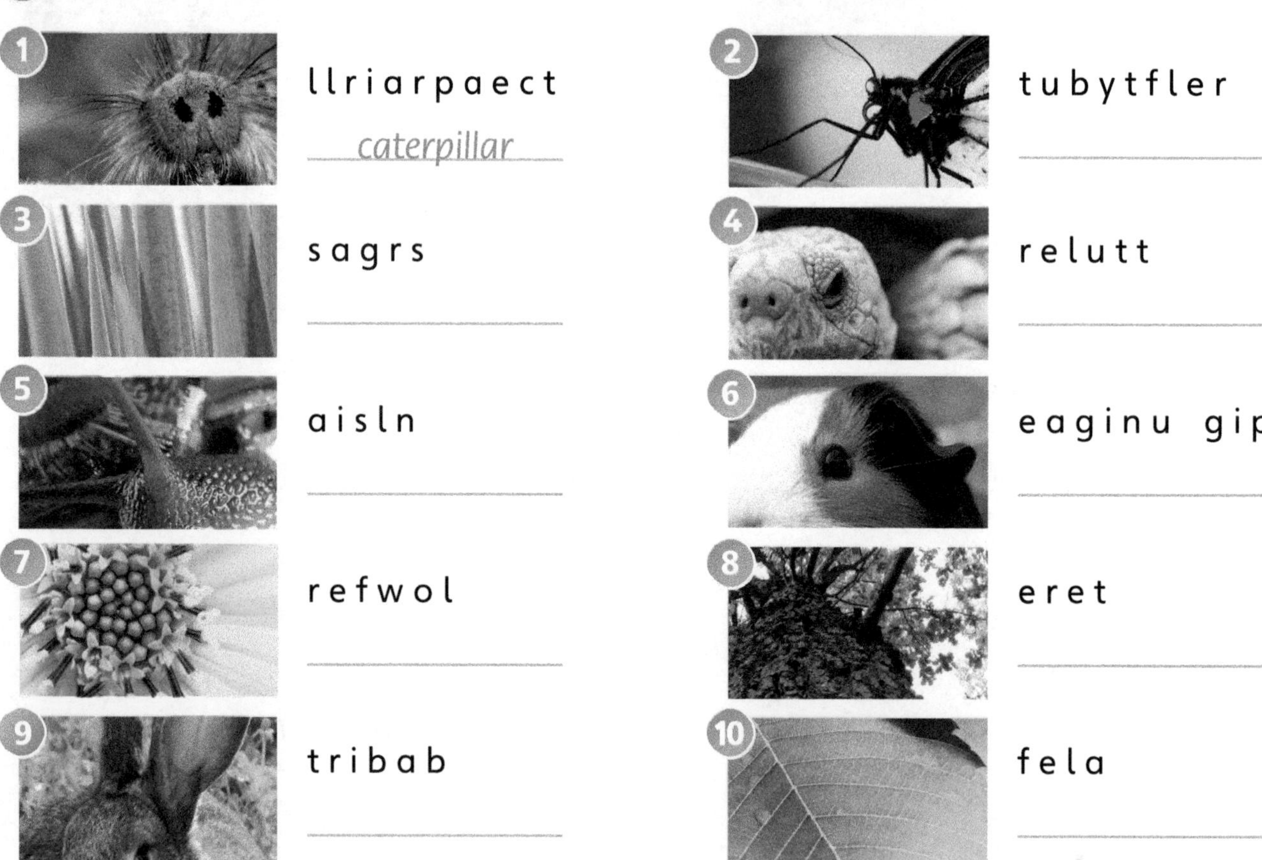

2 Think Write the words from activity 1 on the lists.

Animals	Plants
caterpillar	*grass*

My picture dictionary  Go to page 49: Find and write the new words.

3 Look and circle the words.

1 My / Your pet is big.
2 His / Their pet is small.
3 His / Her pet is brown.
4 Our / My pet is beautiful.
5 My / Our pet is white.

4 Look and complete the sentences. Then color the animals.

~~Her~~ Her His Our	big big ~~small~~ small

1 

Her pet is small and yellow.

2 

______ pet is ______ and gray.

3 

______ pet is ______ and brown.

4 

______ pet is ______ and orange.

5 Look and circle the questions and answers.

1 (What's that?) What are those? — a (It's a snail.) They're snails.

2 What's that? What are those? — b It's a flower. They're flowers.

3 What's that? What are those? — c It's a turtle. They're turtles.

4 What's that? What are those? — d It's a bird. They're birds.

5 What's that? What are those? — e It's a leaf. They're leaves.

6 Look and write the questions and answers.

~~butterflies~~ caterpillar spider trees

1 *What are those?*

They're butterflies.

2 *What's that?*

____

3 ______________________

____

4 ______________________

____

Skills: *Writing*

7 Read the paragraph and write the words.

butterflies leaves ~~small~~ tree white

My favorite bug is a caterpillar. Caterpillars are [1] *small* . I like black and [2] ________ caterpillars. You can see a caterpillar on a [3] ________ . The caterpillar eats the green [4] ________ . Beautiful [5] ________ come from caterpillars.

8 About Me Answer the questions.

1 What's your favorite bug?

My favorite bug is ________

2 What color is it?

____

3 Is it big or small or beautiful?

____

4 Where can you see it?

____

9 About Me Write about your favorite bug.

My favorite bug ________

____

____

____

____

____

____

10 About Me Ask and answer with a friend.

What's your favorite animal?

My favorite animal is a horse.

11 Read and match.

1 Not now, Anna.
2 Sorry, Anna. Thank you.
3 Are those ears and a tail?
4 Can we borrow it, please?

12 Look at activity 11. Answer the questions.

1 What do they see behind the tree? *Ears and a tail.*
2 What animal is behind the tree? ______
3 What animal does Anna have? ______
4 What can they do with it? ______
5 Who is sorry? ______

13 Look and write the questions and answers. Then check the picture that shows the value: respect and listen to others.

~~Can I help?~~ Yes, you can. Thank you. Can I help? Not now.

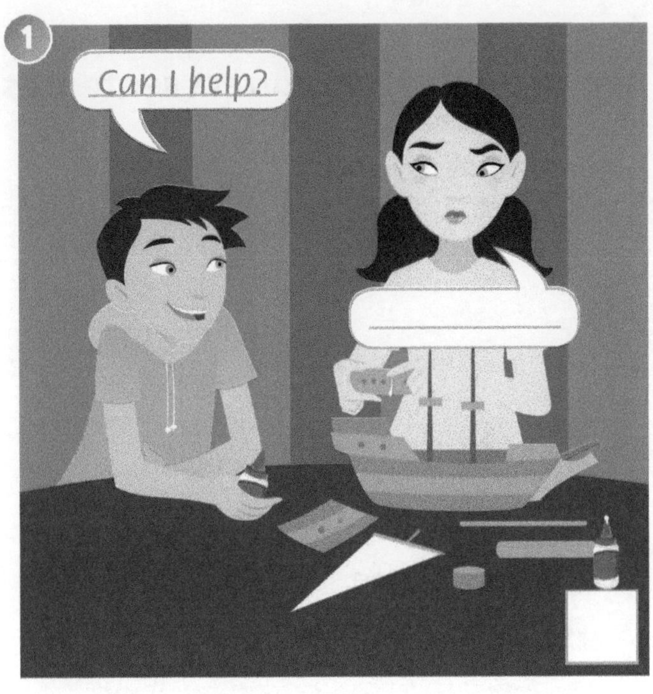

14 Write the words with the same sound in the lists.

~~cake~~ ~~tree~~ paint leaf make jeans sleep eat tail chimpanzee train snake

What types of habitats are there?

1 **Write the names of the habitats. Then circle the two correct sentences.**

desert grassland ~~rain forest~~ tundra

1

It's a hot place.
There are lots of trees and leaves.
Lions live here.

2

It's a cold place.
There are lots of trees.
Bears live here.

3

It's a hot place.
Monkeys live here.
There is a lot of grass.

4

There is little water.
Snakes and spiders live here.
There are lots of fish.

2 **Draw and write about a habitat in your country.**

It's a ______________ place. There are lots of ______________ . ______________ live here.

Evaluation

1 Find and write the words.

1 What's that?
It's a flower.

2 ____________
They're leaves.

3 ____________
They're caterpillars.

4 ____________
It's a butterfly.

5 ____________
It's grass.

2 Look and write the words.

~~My~~ Your Our Their	~~turtle~~ fish rabbit snail	~~small~~ big white green

1 My turtle is small.

2 ______ ______ is ______.

3 ______ ______ is ______.

4 ______ ______ is ______.

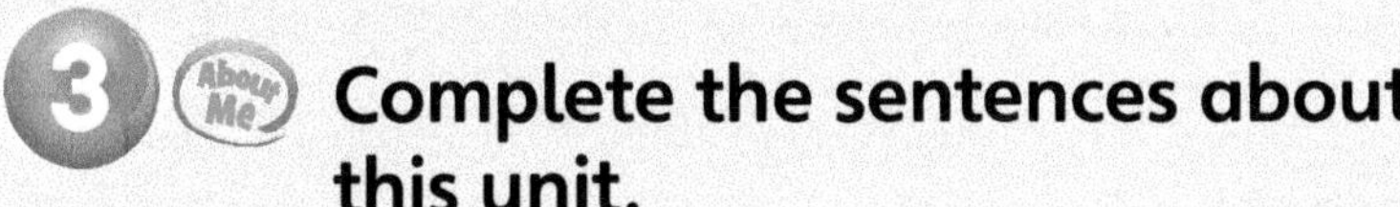

3 About Me Complete the sentences about this unit.

1 I can talk about ____________.

2 I can write about ____________.

3 My favorite part is ____________.

4 Puzzle Guess what it is.

Go to page 53 and circle the answer.

2 At school

1 Look and number the picture.

1 playground
2 gym
3 science lab
4 sports field
5 cafeteria
6 art room
7 library
8 music room
9 reception
10 classroom

2 Think Look at activity 1. Read the sentences and write the words.

1 You can paint pictures in this room ___art room___
2 There are desks and chairs in this room. ______
3 You can eat lunch in this room. ______
4 You have a science class in this room. ______
5 You can run, jump, and dance in this room. ______
6 You go here when you visit the school. ______
7 You can play soccer here. ______
8 You can play outside here. ______
9 You can read books here. ______
10 You can sing here. ______

My picture dictionary  Go to page 50: Find and write the new words.

3 Look and circle the answers.

1 We're / They're on the sports field.

2 We're / They're in the art room.

3 We're / They're in the science lab.

4 We're / They're in the classroom.

4 Look and complete the questions and answers.

1 Where are they ? ________ at reception.

2 Where are ________ ? We're in the library.

3 Where are ________ ? ________ in the gym.

4 Where are ________ ? ________ in the music room.

5 Where are ________ ? ________ on the playground.

5 Read and match.

a They're playing basketball.

b They're playing soccer.

c We're playing basketball.

d We're playing soccer.

6 Look and write the questions and answers.

1 *What are you doing?* *We're*

2 *They're*

3

4

Skills: *Writing*

7 Read the text. Circle the answers to the questions.

My school is small. There are six classrooms, a library, and a big playground. I like the library, but my favorite room is the gym. There are 18 children in my class. My favorite class is English.

1 Is your school big or small?
2 What rooms and places are in your school?
3 What is your favorite room?
4 How many children are in your class?
5 What is your favorite class?

8 About Me Look at activity 7. Answer the questions.

1 My school is ______________________
2 ______________________
3 ______________________
4 ______________________
5 ______________________

9 About Me Write a description of your school.

My school ______________________

____

____

____

____

____

____

10 About Me Ask and answer with a friend.

What's your favorite class?

My favorite class is science.

11 Read and write the words.

Thank you! pick up ~~litter~~ Listen!

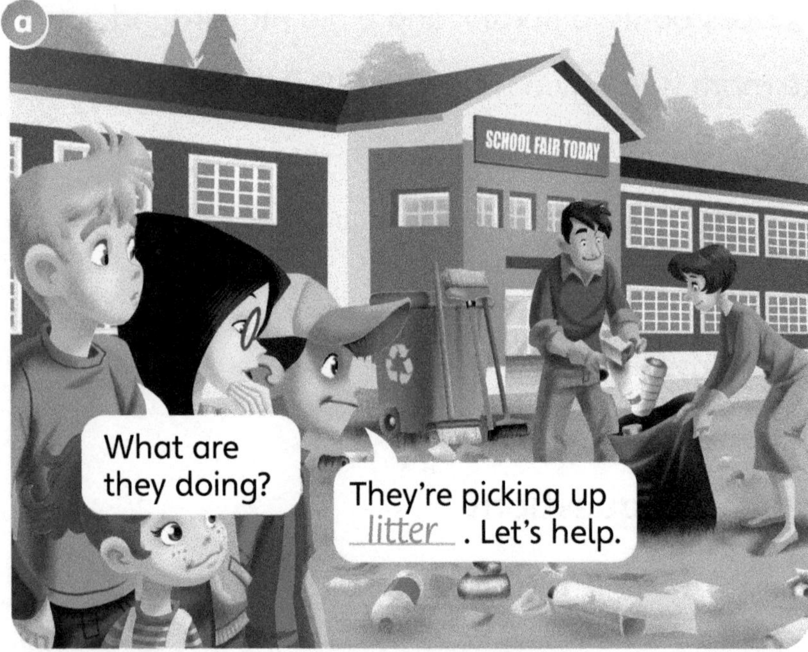
a
SCHOOL FAIR TODAY
What are they doing?
They're picking up litter. Let's help.

b
Hi, Aunt Pat. Can we help?
Yes, please. Can you ______ this litter?

c
Come on, Lily!
Wait! ______ What's that?

d
Thanks for your help! You can have the radio.
SCHOOL FAIR TODAY
______

12 Look at activity 11. Write *yes* or *no*.

1 Dad and Aunt Pat are in the gym. no

2 Aunt Pat is picking up litter. ______

3 The children don't help. ______

4 Lily is listening to the radio. ______

5 Aunt Pat wants the radio. ______

13 Look and check the pictures that show the value: keep your environment clean.

14 Circle the words that sound like *tiger*.

What materials can we recycle?

1 Look and match.

2 Design two recycling bins for your school.

Where is it? ____________________

____

What can children put in it? ____________________

____

Where is it? ____________________

____

What can children put in it? ____________________

____

Evaluation

1 Look and answer the questions.

1 Where are the girls? *They're in the gym.*

2 What are they doing? ____________________

3 Where are the boys? ____________________

4 What are they doing? ____________________

5 Where are the teachers? ____________________

6 What are they doing? ____________________

7 Where are we? ____________________

8 What are we doing? ____________________

2 About Me Complete the sentences about this unit.

1 I can talk about ____________________ .

2 I can write about ____________________ .

3 My favorite part is ____________________ .

3 Puzzle Guess what it is.

Go to page 53 and circle the answer.

Review Units 1 and 2

1 Look and find the numbers. Answer the questions.

1 Where are they? *They're in the science lab.*

2 What are those? ______________________________

3 What's he doing? ______________________________

4 What are those? ______________________________

5 What are they doing? ______________________________

6 Where are they? ______________________________

7 What's that? ______________________________

8 What's that? ______________________________

2 Think Find 11 months ↓ →. Then answer the question.

N	O	V	E	M	B	E	R	T	J	S	F	G	M
A	C	B	Z	A	P	Y	E	J	U	N	E	K	A
W	T	A	Q	Y	N	A	C	I	L	T	B	O	R
B	O	N	J	A	N	U	A	R	Y	S	R	I	C
K	B	U	P	B	T	A	N	G	K	W	U	L	H
D	E	C	E	M	B	E	R	X	A	C	A	G	M
O	R	O	C	G	M	A	I	O	A	P	R	I	L
P	B	Y	A	U	G	U	S	T	W	B	Y	J	D

One month is not in the puzzle. What month is it?

____

3 Look and write the questions.

1 What's her name? It's Kate.
2 ______ It's in May.
3 ______ Her favorite color is pink.
4 Who are they? They're my cousins.
5 ______ They're at the park.
6 ______ They're flying a kite.

4 Look at the photographs in activity 3. Complete the sentences.

1 His T-shirt is yellow. 2 ______ is pink.
3 ______ are blue. 4 ______ is a plane.

5 Think Answer the questions.

a bird a butterfly a caterpillar a cafeteria
February grass ~~a guinea pig~~ a library

1 These eat leaves. What are they? A guinea pig and ______
2 You can eat here. Where is it? ______
3 You can read books here. Where is it? ______
4 These can fly. What are they? ______ and ______
5 This has 8 letters. What month is it? ______
6 This is a plant. What is it? ______

3 School days

1 Write the days of the week.

	nadyMo	ausdeTy	sdaydenWe
	Monday		
Sue			
Dan			

	yhrduTsa	iayFdr	yrtdSaau	ySndua
Sue				
Dan				

2 Look at activity 1. Write *yes* or *no*.

1 She has math on Thursday. yes

2 He has gym on Friday. ______

3 She has art on Monday. ______

4 He has soccer club on Saturday. ______

5 She has computer club on Sunday. ______

3 Look at activity 1. Write the sentences.

1 Monday: She has music, and he has science.

2 Tuesday: ______

3 Wednesday: ______

4 Thursday: ______

5 Friday: ______

My picture dictionary  Go to page 51: Find and write the new words.

4 Look and follow. Then complete the questions and answers.

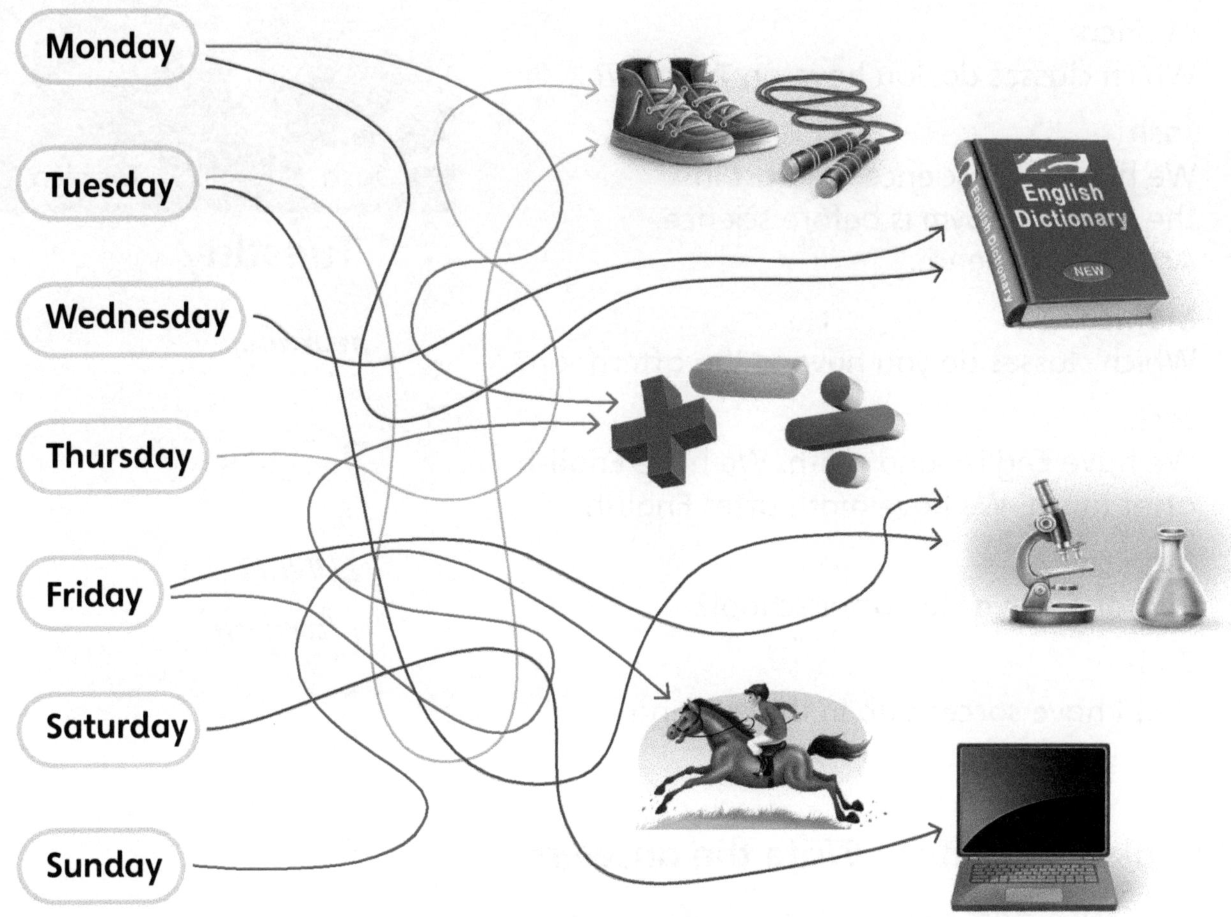

1 Do we have gym on Thursday? Yes, we do.
2 Do we have English on Saturday? ______
3 Do we have math on Monday? ______
4 ______ science on Friday? ______
5 ______ computer club on Sunday? ______
6 ______ horseback riding club on Sunday? ______

5 Look at activity 4. Complete the sentences.

1 We don't have math on Thursday.
2 ______ English on Monday and Wednesday.
3 ______ science on Tuesday and Friday.
4 ______ horseback riding club on Thursday.
5 ______ computer club on Saturday.
6 ______ gym on Monday and Friday.

6 Read and complete Josh's day.

Monica
Which classes do you have on Tuesday?

Josh
We have gym, science, and art in the morning. Gym is before science. Art is after science.

Monica
Which classes do you have in the afternoon?

Josh
We have English and math. We have English after lunch. We have math after English.

Monica
Do you have a club after school?

Josh
Yes, I have soccer club in the evening.

Tuesday

morning

1 __________

2 *science*

3 __________

LUNCH

afternoon

4 __________

5 __________

evening

6 __________

7 Look at activity 6. Write the answers.

1 Which class does Josh have after gym?

He has science after gym.

2 Which class does Josh have after lunch?

____

3 Which class does Josh have before lunch?

____

4 Which class does Josh have before math?

____

8 Choose a day from your schedule. Answer the questions.

1 Which classes do you have in the morning?

I have __________

2 Which classes do you have in the afternoon?

____

3 Do you have a club after school?

____

Skills: *Writing*

9 Read the paragraph and write the words.

horseback club morning ~~Saturday~~ music competitions

My favorite day of the week is [1] *Saturday*. I have a [2] ________ class in the [3] ________. I have photography [4] ________ in the afternoon. In the evening. I have a [5] ________ riding lesson and a dance competition. I like [6] ________.

10 About Me Answer the questions.

1 What's your favorite day of the week?

My favorite day is ________

2 What do you have in the morning?

____

3 What do you have in the afternoon?

____

4 What do you have in the evening?

____

11 About Me Write about your favorite day.

My favorite ________

12 About Me Ask and answer with a friend.

Do you have any clubs this week?

Yes, I have computer club on Thursday.

13 Read and number in order.

a

It's very good, Tom.
What do you think, Max?

b

We can't take a photograph of the painting.
What can we do now?
I have an idea!

c

Is the art gallery open on Saturdays?
Yes, it is.
Come on. Let's go!

d

Be careful!
Are you OK, Tom?
Yes, I'm fine. Don't worry.

e

OK. Here we are.
Now where's the painting?
Over there!

f

What day is it today?
Find this painting.
It's Saturday.
Great! I like art. Let's go to the art gallery.
1

14 Look at activity 13. Answer the questions.

1 Who likes art? Tom.

2 What is open on Saturdays? ______

3 What can't they do? ______

4 What animal is in the painting? ______

5 What does Tom do? ______

15 Look and check the pictures that show the value: be resourceful.

1 

2 

3 

4 

16 Color the words that sound like *goat*. Then answer the question.

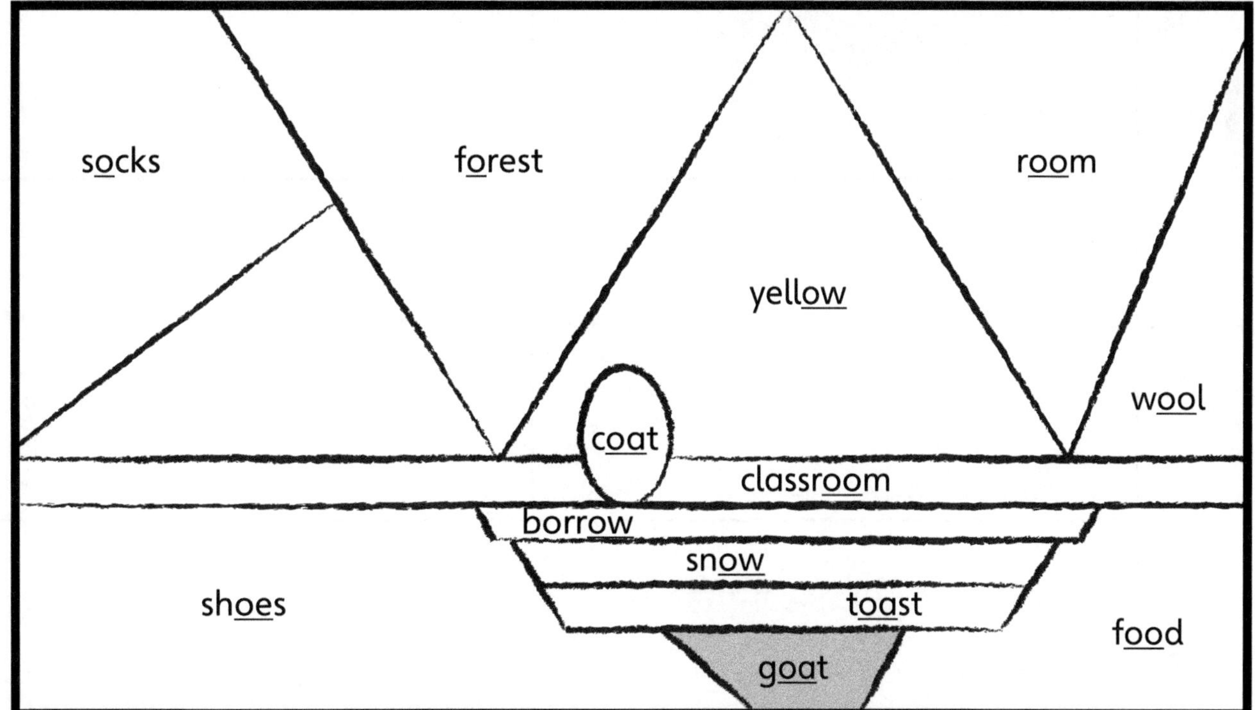

What's in the picture? ______________________

Which animals are nocturnal?

1 Read and check the sentences that are true for nocturnal animals.

1 It finds food and eats at night. ✓
2 It likes running and flying in the day. ☐
3 It likes playing in the evening and at night. ☐
4 It sleeps in the morning and afternoon. ☐

2 Draw and label one animal in each box in the chart. Then write sentences about each animal.

	✓ nocturnal	✗ nocturnal
✗ fly	1 	2
✓ fly	3	4

1 *A scorpion is nocturnal. It can't fly.*
2
3
4

Evaluation

1 Write the days of the week in the diary and answer the questions.

Thursday	**Sa**________
10:00 art 2:00 English test 6:00 soccer club	3:00 gym competition
F________	**S**________
9:00 gym 1:00 science	10:00 photography club 12:00 lunch with Grandma

1 Do you have art on Friday? No, we don't.
2 Do you have art on Thursday? ________
3 Do you have a math test on Thursday? ________
4 Do you have a gym competition on Saturday? ________

2 Look at activity 1. Answer the questions about Emily.

1 Look at Thursday. What does she have in the morning? She has art.
2 Look at Thursday. What does she have in the evening? ________
3 Look at Friday. What does she have in the morning? ________
4 Look at Friday. What does she have in the afternoon? ________
5 Look at Sunday. What does she have before lunch? ________

3 About Me Complete the sentences about this unit.

1 I can talk about ________ .
2 I can write about ________ .
3 My favorite part is ________ .

4 Puzzle Guess what it is.

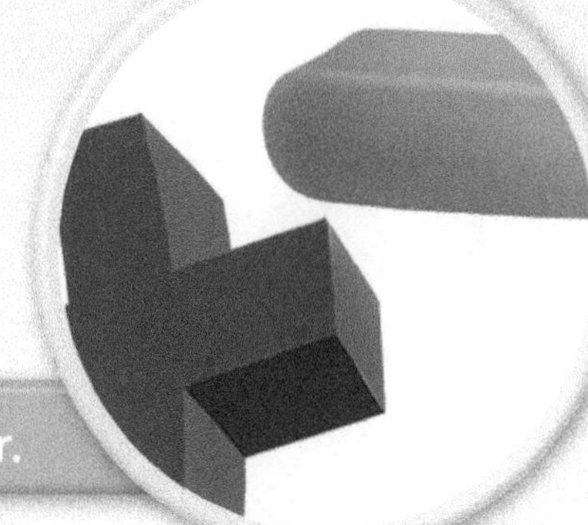

Go to page 53 and circle the answer.

4 My day

1 Look and write the answers.

brush your teeth   get up   go to bed   ~~go to school~~
have breakfast   have dinner   have lunch   take a shower

1 *go to school*

2 ______

3 ______

4 ______

5 ______

6 ______

7 ______

8 ______

2 About Me Look at activity 1. Write six sentences about your day.

1 I *get dressed* in the morning.

2 I ______

3 I ______ in the afternoon.

4 I ______ in the evening.

5 ______

6 ______

My picture dictionary  Go to page 52: Find and write the new words.

3 Read and match.

1 I get dressed at seven o'clock.

2 I go to school at eight o'clock.

3 I eat lunch at twelve o'clock.

4 I go home at three thirty.

5 I eat dinner at seven thirty.

6 I go to bed at nine thirty.

4 Look and complete the sentences.

1 I *get up* at *seven thirty*.

2 I __________ at __________.

3 I __________ at __________.

4 I __________ at __________.

5 I __________ at __________.

6 I __________ at __________.

5 About Me Write sentences and draw the times.

1 I *have breakfast* at __________.

2 I __________ at __________.

3 I __________ at __________.

4 I __________ at __________.

6 Think Read and answer the questions.

Ken: What time do you get up?
Eva: I get up at seven thirty.
Ken: So do I.
Maya: I don't. I get up at seven o'clock.
Maya: What time do you go to bed?
Ken: I go to bed at nine o'clock.
Eva: I don't. I go to bed at eight thirty.
Maya: So do I.

1 Who gets up at seven o'clock? *Maya*
2 Who gets up at seven thirty? ________ and ________
3 Who goes to bed at eight thirty? ________ and ________
4 Who goes to bed at nine o'clock? ________

7 Look and complete the sentences.

1 What time do you have dinner?

So do I. I don't.

2 What time do you have breakfast?

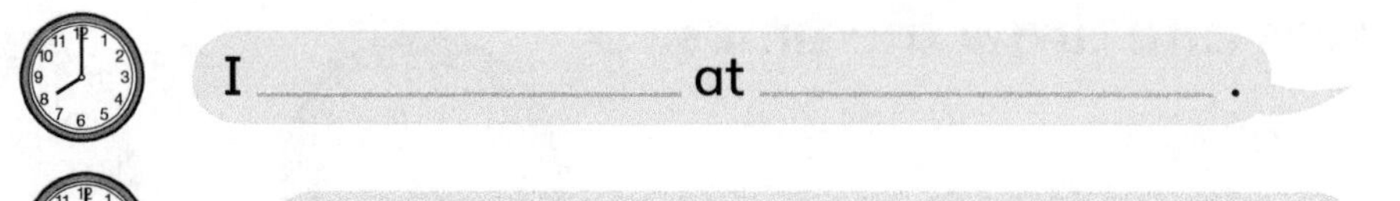

____

8 About Me Ask and answer with two friends.

I get up at …
So do I.
I don't. I get up at …

Skills: Writing

9 Write a questionnaire about a healthy lifestyle. Then ask a friend.

~~have breakfast~~ play outside ~~walk to school~~ ride a bike
~~get up~~ brush your teeth watch TV play sports
play computer games drink orange juice

		Yes / No
1	*Do you have breakfast every day?*	
2	*Do you walk to school in the morning?*	
3	*Do you like getting up early?*	
4		
5		
6		
7		
8		
9		
10		

10 Ask and answer with a friend.

Do you have a healthy lifestyle?

Yes, I do. I walk to school every day.

11 Read and match.

1 I can do the race!	2 Thanks! Swimming is fun!
3 The first prize is a watch!	4 And the winner is ... Lucas!

12 Look at activity 11. Circle the answers.

1 Lucas does ________________ .
a a swimming club b a swimming race c the first prize

2 Lucas thinks swimming is ________________ .
a fun b great c nice

3 Lucas wins ________________ .
a a present b a test c a prize

4 The prize is ________________ .
a a watch b a race c swimming lessons

13 Check the activities that show the value: exercise.

1	do a bike race	✓	2	go to baseball club	
3	take a math test		4	play in a tennis competition	
5	go to bed early		6	go roller-skating	
7	take a shower		8	play sports after school	

14 Circle the words that sound like *blue*.

START!

(blue)	equals	snow	jump	toast	sausage
turn	June	run	goat	excuse	plus
yellow	mouth	shoots	chew	duck	room

FINISH!

What time is it around the world?

1 Look and answer the questions.

1 What time is it in Buenos Aires?

It's *eight o'clock* in the morning.

2 What time is it in London?

It's ______________ in the afternoon.

3 What time is it in Dubai?

It's ______________________________.

4 What time is it in Shanghai?

It's ______________________________.

2 Draw a picture and write sentences.

08:00

1 I ______________ at eight o'clock in the morning.

2 I ______________________________

______________________________.

3 I ______________________________

______________________________.

4 I ______________________________

______________________________.

Evaluation

1 Look and complete the questions and answers.

1 What time do you get up?

I get up at six thirty.

2 What time do you get dressed?

____
____

3 ______________________
____

I go to school at eight o'clock.

4 ______________________
____

I have dinner at half past seven.

5 What time do you brush your teeth?

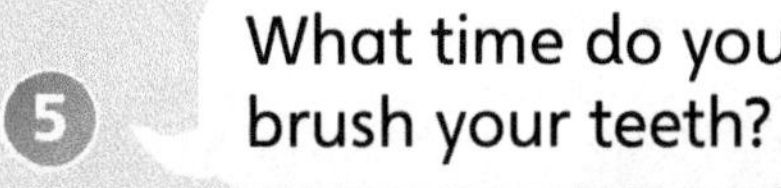

____
____

6 ______________________
____

I go to bed at nine o'clock.

2 Look at activity 1. Write sentences. Start with *So do I* or *I don't*.

1 So do I. I get up at six thirty.
2 ______________________
3 ______________________
4 ______________________
5 ______________________
6 ______________________

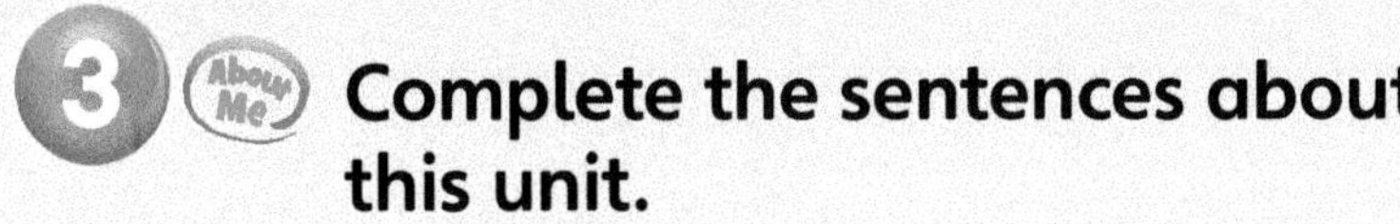

3 Complete the sentences about this unit.

1 I can talk about ______________________ .
2 I can write about ______________________ .
3 My favorite part is ______________________ .

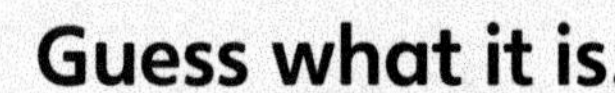

4 Puzzle Guess what it is.

Go to page 53 and circle the answer.

Review Units 3 and 4

1 Look and complete the sentences about my day.

after lunch after school at four o'clock
~~at nine o'clock~~ at six thirty at ten o'clock

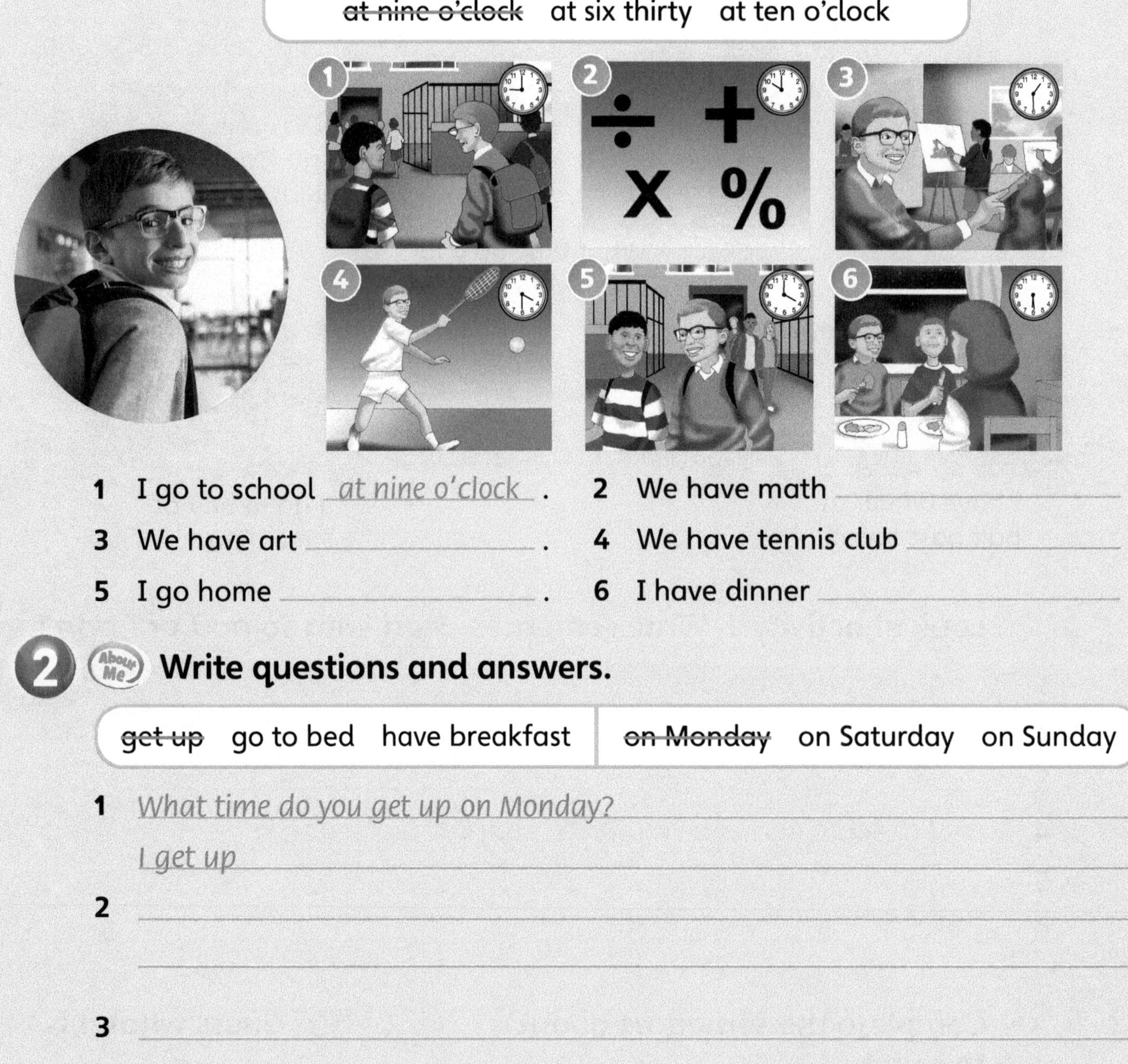

1 I go to school *at nine o'clock* .
2 We have math ______________ .
3 We have art ______________ .
4 We have tennis club ______________ .
5 I go home ______________ .
6 I have dinner ______________ .

2 About Me Write questions and answers.

~~get up~~ go to bed have breakfast | ~~on Monday~~ on Saturday on Sunday

1 *What time do you get up on Monday?*
I get up ______________

2 ______________
____

3 ______________
____

4 ______________
____

3 Find the words ↓ →. Use the words to complete the verbs.

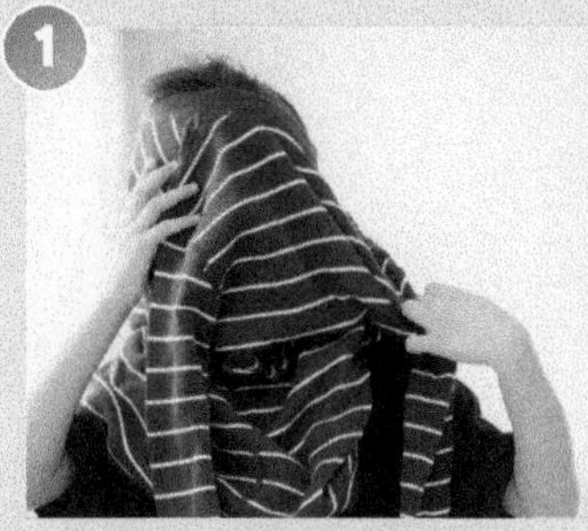

1 get *dressed*

B	H	F	D	T	E	E	T	H
R	W	V	I	P	K	E	X	M
E	L	U	N	C	H	L	U	S
A	O	Y	N	C	G	B	A	C
K	D	R	E	S	S	E	D	H
F	M	E	R	B	O	D	C	O
A	Z	R	W	E	G	H	H	O
S	H	O	W	E	R	Q	R	L
T	X	L	B	A	U	P	C	Z

2 take a ________

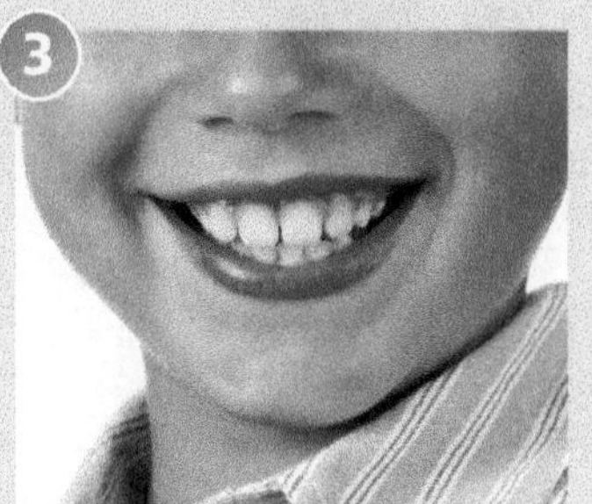

3 brush your ________

4 have ________

5 go to ________

6 have ________

7 have ________

8 go to ________

4  Answer the questions.

1 What day starts with the letter *M*? *Monday*

2 What day has nine letters? ________

3 What day comes after Thursday? ________

4 What day comes before Sunday? ________

5 What day has the letter *H* in it? ________

6 What day sounds like Monday? ________

7 Put these letters in order: YADSUTE. ________

Welcome

Lucas ~~Anna~~ Max Tom Lily

Anna

March December ~~January~~ August April October
June November May February July September

January	F _ _ _ _ _ _ _	M _ _ _ _
A _ _ _ _	M _ _	J _ _ _
J _ _ _	A _ _ _ _ _	S _ _ _ _ _ _ _ _
O _ _ _ _ _ _	N _ _ _ _ _ _ _	D _ _ _ _ _ _ _

1 In the yard

snail guinea pig caterpillar turtle ~~butterfly~~
tree flower grass rabbit leaf

2 At school

reception library sports field classroom gym music room
cafeteria ~~art room~~ playground science lab

art room

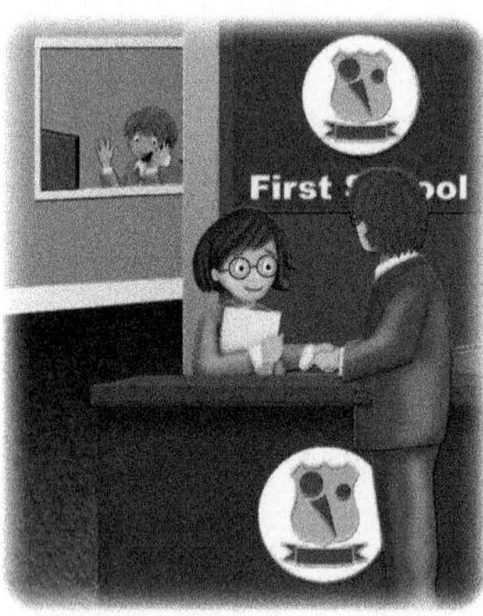

3 School days

Saturday Tuesday ~~Monday~~ Thursday
Sunday Wednesday Friday

M o n d a y

T _ _ _ _ _ _

W _ _ _ _ _ _ _ _

T _ _ _ _ _ _ _

F _ _ _ _ _

S _ _ _ _ _ _ _

S _ _ _ _ _

4 My day

go to school | get up | take a shower | have breakfast | get dressed
have lunch | go home | have dinner | ~~brush your teeth~~ | go to bed

My puzzle

1 Find the words ↓ →. Use the colored letters to answer the question.

P	G	L	I	B	R	A	R	Y	A	R	C	U	B
I	Q	E	R	T	G	Y	J	K	E	L	P	V	E
N	L	A	B	U	T	T	E	R	F	L	Y	U	V
E	B	Z	M	S	W	L	H	B	G	T	D	A	M
A	M	N	F	O	T	D	W	B	I	I	S	O	A
P	G	O	A	O	S	H	O	W	E	R	H	X	T
P	A	A	N	M	G	I	R	C	M	Q	E	Z	H
L	S	G	N	H	K	L	U	Y	O	O	L	P	M
E	M	U	A	N	T	U	E	R	N	S	L	L	Y
X	V	I	E	B	G	H	Y	O	P	W	F	R	Y
D	O	T	H	E	D	I	S	H	E	S	O	K	R
J	K	A	S	K	V	B	Y	U	W	E	T	R	E
M	I	R	W	T	E	C	J	F	H	A	N	N	A

Q: What are two things people can't eat before breakfast?

A: _ _ _ _ _ and _ _ _ _ _ _

Story fun

1 Match the objects to the words. Then match the words to the story units they come from.

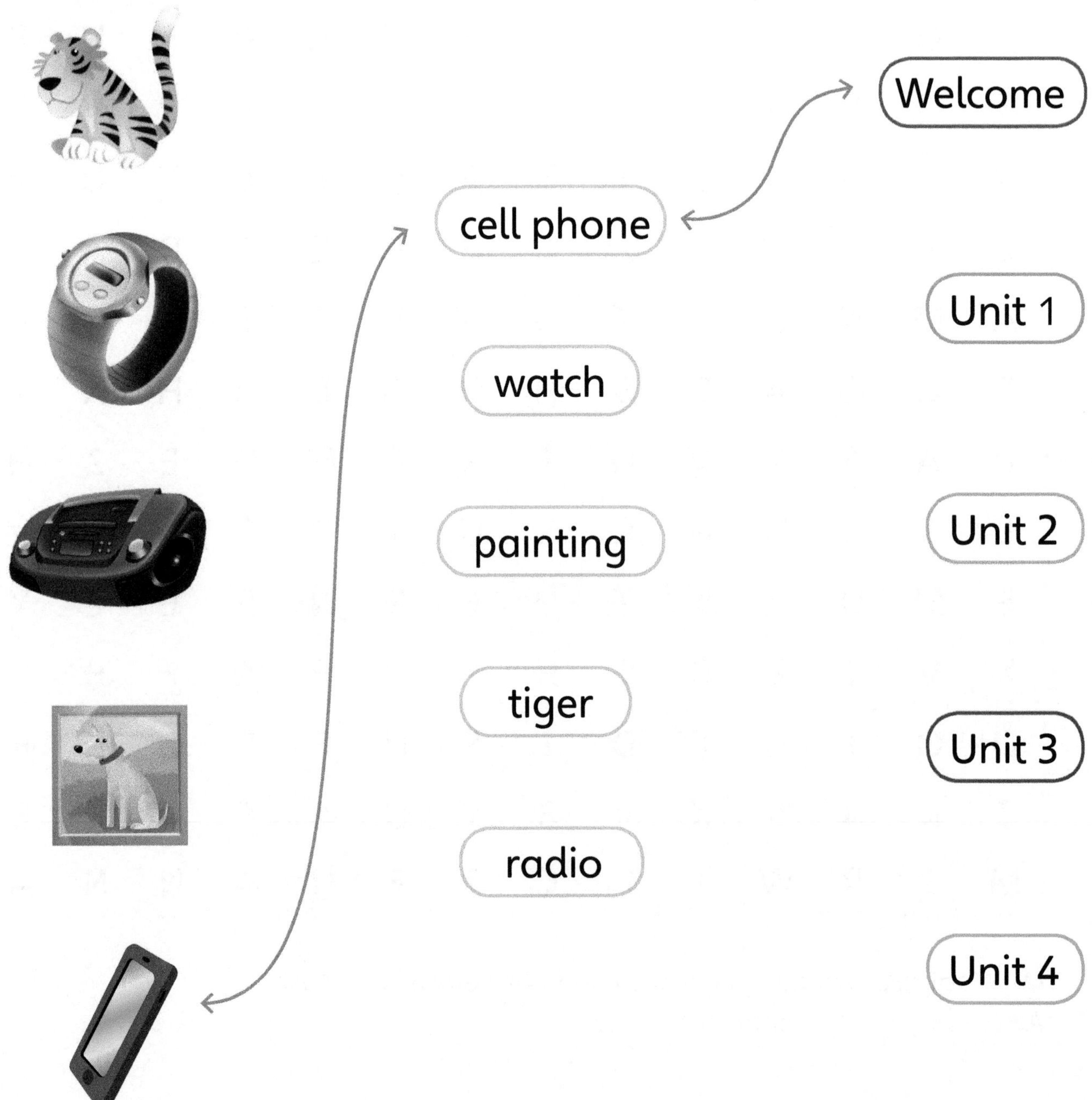

1 Write the numbers in the box of the objects.

Acknowledgments

Many thanks to everyone in the excellent team at Cambridge University Press & Assessment in Spain, the UK, and India.

The authors and publishers would like to thank the following contributors:
Blooberry Design: concept design, cover design, book design
Hyphen: publishing management, page make-up
Ann Thomson: art direction
Gareth Boden: commissioned photography
Jon Barlow: commissioned photography
Ian Harker: class audio recording
John Marshall Media: "Grammar fun" recordings
Robert Lee, Dib Dib Dub Studios: song and chant composition
Vince Cross: theme tune composition
James Richardson: arrangement of theme tune
Phaebus: "CLIL" video production
Kiki Foster: "Look!" video production
Bill Smith Group: "Grammar fun" and story animations
Sounds Like Mike Ltd: "Grammar Fun" video production

The authors and publishers acknowledge the following sources of copyright material and are grateful for the permissions granted. While every effort has been made, it has not always been possible to identify the sources of all the material used, or to trace all copyright holders. If any omissions are brought to our notice, we will be happy to include the appropriate acknowledgements on reprinting and in the next update to the digital edition, as applicable.

Key: U = Unit.

Student's Book

Photography

The following photos are sourced from Getty Images:
U0: kali9/E+; zianlob/iStock/Getty Images Plus; Martin Harvey/The Image Bank; jaroon/E+; IndiaPix/IndiaPicture; Jose Luis Pelaez Inc/DigitalVision; XiXinXing; damircudic/E+; **U1:** Tatiana Lobanova/iStock/Getty Images Plus; szefei/iStock/ Getty Images Plus; Cavan Images; ivanmateev/iStock/Getty Images Plus; Darrell Gulin/The Image Bank; Antagain/E+; arlindo71/E+; a.collectionRF/amana images; Prasit photo/Moment; MILATAS; Corey Hochachka/Design Pics;
U2: MichaelDeLeon/E+; MNStudio/iStock/Getty Images Plus; Pablo Alberto Velasco Ibarra/EyeEM; Janie Airey/DigitalVision; Jupiterimages/Stockbyte; Brand X Pictures/Stockbyte; Sergiy Trofimov Photography/Moment; Mint Images/Mint Images; Huber\u0026 Starke/Corbis; globestock/E+; Andersen Ross Photography Inc/DigitalVision; Klaus Vedfelt/DigitalVision; **U3:** Bartosz Hadyniak/E+; Daniel R Monroe/500px; Mike Kemp/Tetra images; Lane Oatey/Blue Jean Images/blue jean images; WIN-Initiative/Neleman/Stone; The Good Brigade/DigitalVision; MichaelDeLeon/E+; **U4:** Stephen Simpson/Stone; Juanmonino/E+; nehopelon/ iStock/Getty Images Plus; Barry Downard; Shy Al Britanni/arabianEye; Rosemary Calvert/Photographer's Choice; Photodisc; THEPALMER/E+; Milko/E+; Marc Romanelli/Tetra images.

The following photos are sourced from other libraries:
U0: serhi000111/Shutterstock; TongRo Images/Alamy; KPG-Payless/Shutterstock; Robert Daly/OJO Images Ltd/Alamy; Robert Harding World Imagery/Alamy; Martyn Goddard/Alamy; Jaroslaw Grudzinski/Shutterstock; Galyna Andrushko/ Shutterstock; Nicha/Shutterstock; konzeptm/Shutterstock; Calin Tatu/ Shutterstock; iBird/Shutterstock; nodff/Shutterstock; antpkr/Shutterstock; Lillya Kulianionak/Shutterstock; **U1:** crazychris84/Shutterstock; Sergii Figurnyi/ Shutterstock; ARTSILENSE/Shutterstock; Ivan Cholakov/Shutterstock; nrey/ Shutterstock; Michael Warwick/Shutterstock; Matt Jeppson/Shutterstock; carlos Villoch-MagicSea.com/Alamy; jajaladdawan/Shutterstock; FloridaStock/ Shutterstock; Ernie Janes/Alamy; retiles4all/Shutterstock; liubomirt/Shutterstock; Ryan M. Bolton/Shutterstock; James Urbach/Purestock/SuperStock/Alamy; James Laurie/Shutterstock; Toshe Ognjanov/Shutterstock; Monkey Business Images/ Shutterstock; Liudmila P. Sundikova/Shutterstock; Brocreative/Shutterstock; Laszlo Halasi/Shutterstock; FLPA/Alamy; Luciano Candisani/Minden Pictures/Alamy; Carole-Anne Fooks/Alamy; **U2:** Kike Calvo/National Geographic Society/Corbis; Mark Herreid/Shutterstock; Gabe Palmer/Alamy; Antenna/fStop Images GmbH/ Alamy; Tanja Giessler/fStop Images GmbH/Alamy; Lightspring/Shutterstock; Marquisphoto/Shutterstock; Ulrich Mueller/Shutterstock; italianestro/ Shutterstock; pixinoo/Shutterstock; Phovoir/Shutterstock; criben/Shutterstock; Sally and Richard Greenhill/Alamy; Peter Bennett/Citizen of the Planet/Alamy; JLP/Jose L. Pelaez/Corbis; **U3:** Trevor Smith/Alamy; IE360/Cultura Creative/Alamy; Christine Langer-Pueschel/Shutterstock; igor kisselev/Shutterstock; Air Images/ Shutterstock; Julian Abrams-VIEW/Alamy; ThomasLENNE/Shutterstock; Monkey Business Images/Shutterstock; sianc/Shutterstock; PT Images/Shutterstock; D.Hurst/Alamy; Robert Harding World Imagery/Alamy; Douglas Noblet/All Canada Photos/Alamy; Julian W/Shutterstock; Sandy Hedgepeth/Shutterstock; jakit17/Shutterstock; Dennis W Donohue/Shutterstock; DnDavis/Shutterstock; Moodboard Stock Photography/Alamy; Kim Taylor/Nature Picture Library/Alamy; Theerapol Pongkangsananan/Shutterstock; Ziggylives/Shutterstock; Roman Malanchuk/Shutterstock; rdonar/Shutterstock; **U4:** Kristian Buus/Alamy; Peter Titsmuss/Alamy; Judith Collins/Alamy; Peter Titmus/Alamy; Jill Chen/Shutterstock; Zoonar GmbH/Alamy; Shailth/Shutterstock; Flip Nicklin/Minden Pictures/Alamy; DYLAN MARTINEZ/Reuters/Corbis; Finnbarr Webster/Alamy; Andrew Wood/ Alamy; Steve Heap/Shutterstock; Tetra Images/Alamy; Cultura Creative/Alamy; Red Images, LLC/Alamy; Sabina Jane Blackbird/Alamy; Nuchylee/Shutterstock; Monkey Business Images/Shutterstock; chonrawit boonprakob/Shutterstock.

Workbook

Photography

The following photos are sourced from Getty Images:
U0: Tatiana Lobanova/iStock/Getty Images Plus; **U3:** Randy Plett/Getty; Bartosz Hadyniak/E+; GlobalStock/iStock/Getty Images Plus; Heide Benser/The Image Bank; Daniel R Monroe/500px; **U4:** Fuse/Corbis; nehopelon/iStock/Getty Images Plus; JGI/Jamie Grill/Tetra images.

The following photos are sourced from other libraries:
U0: Tongro Image Stock/Alamy; pirita/Shutterstock; Rob Walls/Alamy; KPG-Payless/Shutterstock; Martyn Goddard/Alamy; homydesign/Shutterstock; worker/ Shutterstock; **U1:** Premaphotos/Alamy; Johan Larson/Shutterstock; sevenke/ Shutterstock; Roman Sigaev/Shutterstock; Alexander Mak/Shutterstock; E. Spek/ Shutterstock; hramovnick/Shutterstock; vaklav/Shutterstock; Petro Perutskyi/ Shutterstock; Jaroslav74/Shutterstock; liubomir/Shutterstock; Laszio Halasi/ Shutterstock; Vetapi/Shutterstock; **U2:** Kike Calvo/National Geographic Society/ Corbis; Amy Myers/Shutterstock; Monkey Business Images/Shutterstock; Adrian Sherratt/Alamy; wavebreakmedia/Shutterstock; Mark Herreid/Shutterstock; neelsky/Shutterstock; Sergii Figurnyi/Shutterstock; Korionov/Shutterstock; Santi S/Shutterstock; Elena Elisseeva/Shutterstock; Edwin Butter/Shutterstock; TSpider/Shutterstock; dotshock/Shutterstock; stable/Shutterstock; Lightspring/ Shutterstock; Radu Bercan/Shutterstock; SuperStock/Purestock/Alamy; Cultura/ Alamy; **U3:** ThomasLENNE/Shutterstock; Adam Jones/Visuals Unlimited/Corbis; Fuse/Corbis; **U4:** Kristian Buus/Alamy; Shailth/Shutterstock; Mile Atanasov/ Shutterstock; Hero Images Inc./Corbis; Offscreen/Shutterstock; Roger Jegg - Fotodesign-Jegg.de/Shutterstock; David Pimborough/Shutterstock; By Ian Miles-Flashpoint Pictures/Alamy; Andrea Heselton/Alamy; tamata/Shutterstock; Greg Newton/Arcaid Images/Alamy; Adrian Cook/Alamy.

Front Cover Photography by Olena Kuzina/iStock/Getty Images Plus.

Illustrations

Aphik; A Corazon Abierto; Luke Newell; Marcus Cutler; Mark Duffin; Pablo Gallego; Brian Lee; Gareth Conway (Bright Agency); Graham Kennedy; Humberto Blanco (Sylvie Poggio); Ilias Arahovitis (Beehive Illustration); Monkey Feet; Simon Walmesley.